Joseph Edkins

The Evolution of the Chinese Language

As Exemplifying the Origin and Growth of Human Speech

Joseph Edkins

The Evolution of the Chinese Language
As Exemplifying the Origin and Growth of Human Speech

ISBN/EAN: 9783337166205

Printed in Europe, USA, Canada, Australia, Japan

Cover: Foto ©Thomas Meinert / pixelio.de

More available books at **www.hansebooks.com**

THE EVOLUTION

OF THE

CHINESE LANGUAGE

AS EXEMPLIFYING THE ORIGIN AND GROWTH
OF HUMAN SPEECH

BY

JOSEPH EDKINS, D.D.

AUTHOR OF

" RELIGION IN CHINA," " CHINESE BUDDHISM," "GRAMMAR OF THE
MANDARIN LANGUAGE," "CHINA'S PLACE IN PHILOLOGY," ETC.

Reprinted from the "Journal of the Peking Oriental Society," 1887

LONDON
TRÜBNER & CO., 57 & 59 LUDGATE HILL
1888

PREFACE.

CHINA is separated by the ocean, by deserts, and by mountain chains from all nations possessed of original literatures, and her language is more isolated than any other form of human speech studied by philologists. While Chinese has been brought to a high degree of excellence by a people devoted to literary pursuits, it remains possessed of a primitive order of words, and a monosyllabic structure. These peculiarities give it a claim to be a direct descendant of the mother tongue of humanity, but it is not itself that mother tongue. Nor, so far as can be seen, is any other language having a wide area, whether near or far away, a descendant of the Chinese. Further, it may be said that there is no other language, or family of language, which can be more reasonably assumed to be the speech first used in the world's grey morning than can the Chinese. None has proceeded on its course more naturally and gradually, or suffered less by violent inversions in the arrangement of roots. Hence, Chinese is regarded in this essay as the equivalent of the primeval language, and is treated as forming with that language, as seen through a long perspective, a consolidated unity.

There are many reasons why the great Asiatic languages which have literatures should all have sprung from one stem, which may have been current in Asia ten thousand years ago. The power to produce a literature, for example, is hereditary, and the having that power points to a common origin. But this book does not enter on the question. The believer in one original language, and the believer in several, may alike read it without finding any contradiction of their views. Its aim is of a humbler kind. It takes advantage of the simplicity in structure, and regularity in change, belonging to the speech of one people, and proceeds to look steadily at the problem how did that people become possessed of their peculiar speech. The evolution of this one language is kept before the mind exclusively in order that attention may be fixed upon the physiological phenomena present in the origin and growth of speech. Special prominence is given to the priority of the lips in making letters when compared with the teeth, tongue and palate, involving as a consequence the priority of labial roots over others. The necessary activity of the hand in root-making is described as being of high importance in originating pronouns, and the distinction between verbs and nouns, as well as in marking dimensions in space and opposition in qualities.

The hand and the vocal organs are ministers of the mind in creating language, and they are able to do so by physiological connections and agencies. Language is a physical science, as shown many years ago by Professor Max Müller, and belongs to physiology. Words may be looked at as the successive products of the vocal organs, and syntax is the order of their occurrence. But so far as language is physiological, the history of one language is the history of every other. The identity of an eastern and western word or phonetic law may be merely the identity of physiological processes, here on Asiatic, and there on European soil. But in the earliest ages the derivation of languages from unity being the hypothesis which has most probability on its side, the philology of separate families is fused in one general philology, in which families and individual languages cease to be distinguished. Separation soon followed, and was attended by great changes, and primeval grammar was revolutionized by inversions in many linguistic families; the wanderings of races had the effect of making many old words obsolete, and bringing new ones to the front. War and conquest, mingling strange races, profoundly modified the vocabularies of each. Mountains, plains, and the sea, affected some nations fundamentally, producing indelible impressions on their languages. The habits of men in society, of necessity, become reflected in their modes of speech. The chasm dividing the idiom of this and that nation becomes deeper and wider in proportion as the countries they occupy are farther apart, and their modes of life more unlike. But it may be worth considering whether, by the help of physiological light, the path back to a common unity in roots can or cannot be discovered, and whether also it is not possible to learn the causes of the diversity in the arrangement of words which different languages exhibit when compared with each other. That race which is the most energetic of all has spread itself over an enormous area, and originated a host of mighty historical nations which have enshrined their achievements in undying literatures. It is precisely among these peoples that the laws of syntax vary most, and they vary also according to a certain law of geographical contiguity, so that if the order of syntax of one of them be known, the syntax of their former conquerors or neighbours may be known also. The conclusion to be drawn is, that when races mingle, the syntax of the stronger or the more numerous or the more cultivated wins a gradual victory. The recognition of this view by Bishop Caldwell in his notice of my "China's Place in Philology" * seems to show that it will soon be carefully considered by philologists, for he stands first in comparative studies in the modern languages of India.

While evolution is the law that controls the progress of language and unity, the source from which it proceeds, it ought not to be objected that on this showing there is no divine agency in language. Language has become what it is because God would have humanity, His child, cultivate the gift of reason, employ in fulfilment of their best purpose his vocal organs, and in doing so frame for himself a system of audible symbols destined to be the vehicle of elevated moral.

* Caldwell's "Comparative Grammar of the Dravidian or South Indian Language," second edition, pp. 55, 56.

and intellectual instruction, so that he might rise for ever in the scale of progressive excellence. Some in these days have given up the phrase final causes, they have in this been too hasty. There is, for instance, in the evolution of language a remarkably convincing example of a final cause. Man's vocal organs have been so constructed by the divine workman in the use of evolutionary processes, that, in acquiring speech, their possessor might become capable of knowing and serving his Maker, of a virtuous life of research in science and philosophy. Here is, indeed, a final cause worth noting for the vastness of area which it embraces. History, philanthropy, thought, education, civilized usages, laws, religion, divine revelation, would have been impossible, but for the gift of language to mankind. So much I say here to indicate the ultimate bearings of the argument of this book and meet objections beforehand.

J. E.

PEKING,
    September 21, 1887.

CONTENTS.

—◦◦◦—

I.

II.

III.

Rounded vowels.—Primary and wide vowels.—Causes of variation in letters. Change of shape in the adjoining region.—Migration from without inwards, caused by economy of energy.—Muscular rest.— Change of place in muscular activity.—Growth in civilization demands more vocal variety.

IV.

Tones and distinction of surd and sonant entirely in the larynx.— Old middle dialect.—Double pitch with interval of a second.—Time when this interval was adopted.—Inflections of voice.—Three tones in B.C. 800.—New tone first applied to words with vowel finals.—The two old tones had nasal and mute endings respectively.—The new tone replaced lost mutes.—Four tones from 5th to 11th cent.—Intonations took the place of sonant initials and surd finals.—Later evolution of tones.—Earlier evolution of letters.—Both processes slow.—Change began at the lips.—Tones in English, Greek, Latin, how far analogous.

V.

In old Chinese the syllable has commonly a consonant at both ends. —The noise of collision imitated and shaped into a word.—Change of m to b, to f, to p, to p aspirated.—Examples of change from m and b to d, g, n, ng.—Noise of collision, of wind, of humming.—Change of p to t and ch.—Extent of changes in 1000 years.—Direction of change from lips and teeth inward.—Exceptions.—Labial initials mark the oldest words.—Etymologies to be sought in labials.—Six proofs of change from labials to dental and guttural letters.

VI.

Mouth gestures.—Opening, rounding, closing of lips.—Interjections. —Hand gestures.—All acts might be the basis of words.—Each needed to be distinguished by some mark.—Foot gestures.—Each sound heard needed some vocal mark.—No words from eye gestures.—Words to see from cutting. — Differentiating element in words. — Demonstratives early needed.—Sound is the nutriment of a new word.—Call of birds. —Natural sound added to name of hand.—Words are made by derivation.—Derivation by letters shifting from lip to tongue and palate.— Separate creation of roots impracticable. — All roots derivatives. — Aspiration as a mode of derivation. — Place of gesture in making words. — New words are the divided parts of old words. — Head gestures.—Nodding.—Marks.—Counters used before the invention of writing.

VII.

Oldest roots dates from the labial age.—Many roots originated in the dental age, that of early civilization.—Guttural age followed.— Not finished at the invention of writing B.C. 2500.—The tone age began B.C. 1800.—The age of the modern language A.D. 1000.

VIII.

Sporadic novelties.—Tendency to imitation.—Emphasis on special sense—Weariness felt in repetition.—Muscles find rest in change.— Attention to certain particulars in objects.—Limitation of sense.— New wants of civilization.—Effect of fashion.—Fancied cacophony.— Obsolete words have laws of their own.—Honorific principles.—Compensation.—Phonetic decay resulting from law of least exertion.—One letter in a word changing, affects its neighbour.

IX.

Roots for pointing and the hand.—The hand and the demonstrative pronoun are identical.—How words for right and left, before and behind, above and below, were formed.—Sending out and pushing.— Efficiency of the hand in word-making increased by a staff or cutting instrument. — The hand a measurer. — Rubbing. — Brushing. — The evolution of the substantive verb.—The finals *p, t, k*, mark commands and assertions.—*M, n, ng* used for unaccentuated narrative.

X.

Nouns and verbs not divided at first.—When required to be divided the mind assigned special vocal marks sufficient to distinguish them. —The branching out of verbs into species.—All verbs are nouns, the Chinese verb especially so.—It is a noun with movement in space and time.—Transitive force assigned to verbs subsequently to their occupying a certain position.—No inversions of position in primitive speech. —Causative.—Passive.—Instrumental.—Past tense.—Case particles of nouns.—Early example.

*** For evolution of substantive verb with affirmative and negative varieties see pp. 65, 66.

XI.

The use of the hand in pairing adjectives.—Adjectives are nouns and verbs modified.—Words for bright derived from an aperture, and the aperture from the hand that makes it.—Words for dark derived from the hand covering objects.—Words for beautiful from softness. —Words denoting space, distinction, all from the hand.—Adjectives denoting colours taken from coloured objects.—Adjectives meaning "real" formed from the substantive verb affirming.—All adjectives are nouns.—Comparison of adjectives.

XII.

Explanation of ten.—A *bundle* of objects corresponding in number to the fingers.—Unity is a finger or a counter.—Two is a verb to *cut*.— Four and eight are verbs to *cut* also.—Five from *cutting* or from the hands placed *opposite*.—Six is an *addition*.—Seven is the left forefinger *touching* and pressing.—Nine is *deficiency* of one.—Hundred is *chief*.— Thousand in the leader going *before*.—Myriad is an adjective *full*.— The ordinal is a demonstrative, *this*.

XIII.

XIV.

XV.

XVI.

ERRATA.

Page 7, line 3 from bottom *read* " adverbs of time."

„ 23 „ 10 from bottom after "vowel" *insert* the words : " The Chinese in tables of old sounds set down the vowels as sonants and surds; hence the difference was one of pitch, and so we learn that in the Tang," &c.

„ 27 „ 10, *read* "*ki* with the even tone meant."

EVOLUTION

OF THE

CHINESE LANGUAGE.

I.

A language like the Chinese would be formed in a community sufficiently large to allow of new words obtaining currency. Such a community would before being possessed of language make use of gestures and a certain success would be attained in the communication of thought in this way. To gestures would be added cries indicative of certain feelings. The mouth therefore would very early acquire importance even before the full complement of the vowels and consonants were in use. At first the language would consist of a few cries and the gestures of the head, the lips, the hands and the feet. But soon the mind acting on the vocal organs became conscious of new power. It perceived that words, or vocal signs of ideas could be used to express thoughts and emotions. This led to the creation of letters as the materials of which words are made. Beginning with the use of those formed by the lips, man went forward employing others without too long delays, till from the lips to the glottis all the necessary sounds were formed.

Those **cries** which were a part of the apparatus of the primeval language of gesture, became the foundation of the language of letters, words and sentences, and since from gesture to word there would necessarily be a gradation from the less perfect to the more perfect, the creation of letters could not but begin with the lips which were already in full use in the gestures by which the first men attempted to converse with each other.

The union of gesture with labial letters may be illustrated in the following manner. God endowed man with an intellectual and spiritual nature. The mind thus originated grappled at first with the difficulties of gesture language in the attempt to form a medium of communication. Man was then constantly rising in the intellectual scale and gestures would be improved by vocal sounds which would become daily more distinct and gradually assume the shape of intelligible words. The opening and closing of the lips without voice was insufficient. The mind supplemented these movements by vocal utterance. There would be, let us say, the *a* in father. It was differentiated by the labial check or quick closing of the lips. If the nose passage was open, this gave the sound *m*. If closed, it gave *b*. Thus the work of creating letters began with the closing of the lips which was quite a familiar feature in the gesture language already existing. The union of voice with the closing and opening of the lips was the commencement of audible language. It was when this took place for the first time to symbolize an idea that the first human word was spoken.

We naturally feel a curiosity to know through how long a time language has been in existence. Roughly we may say that the time when language commenced would be after the glacial period when the first traces of fossil man are found. Here I may be permitted to refer to the conclusion of Sir J. W. Dawson in his Points of Contact (1) between Revelation and Natural Science. He estimates the end of the glacial period by the rate of erosion of the Niagara River which is now seven miles from Lake Ontario. The Falls of Niagara carry away three feet of rock of the glacial period each year, as known by the Geodetic Surveys of the State of New York. This is the rate at which the Falls recede from the shores of Lake Ontario and with this as a basis Sir W. Dawson estimates the first appearance of man on the earth as having taken place about seven thousand years ago in the temperate zone.

Chinese may be assumed to have gone through something near a career of this length and less would not suffice probably for the requirements of so complex a development as that of this language. It would be of no advantage to view Chinese as a derived language, for the mother tongue from which it could be descended is unknown. A better course is to derive it as we best may from nature, to place ourselves in front of the circumstances of the early world and attempt to realize the position of the first men from the point of view supplied by the existing Chinese language with its roots and its grammar. The aim of this essay is to carry out this idea in the limited are a of this one language, ignoring for the time the question of its relationship with other modes of speech.

Let us imagine a gutta percha tube made to represent the air and voice passage of the human mouth. There is a great bend at the throat. The perpendicular part of the tube commences in the lungs. The voice originates there or rather it will be enough to say in the larynx through which the air arrives at the mouth. The muscular contractions round the larynx expel the air in successive

(1) London 1886. Sir J. W. Dawson is President of the British Association for the advancement of Science for 1887—8.

puffs. The puffs of sound pass through the glottis on their way and may be viewed as high or low, loud or weak, even or inflected, according to the swiftness, slowness and variability of the vibrations which produce the puffs of air. If we breathe into our tube slowly weak sounds are produced. If we breathe quickly and with force loud sounds are produced. Rapid vibrations make a high and shrill sound. Vibrations few in number make a low and gentle sound. Variability in the pulsations makes inflections in sound. Here is our basis for the Chinese tones and the upper and lower series of sounds. All this takes place within the larynx before the vocal air has passed the triangular door called the glottis and turned the corner on its way to the mouth and nose.

In the mouth there are three barriers through which the air has to pass and our gutta percha tube represents them. There is also a tongue which swells and contracts, advances and retreats with marvellous flexibility. At the hindmost barrier, _k, g_ and _ng_ are formed by the back of the tongue and the soft palate. The tongue moves upward towards the palate and contracts the sound passage in various degrees. The front of the tongue is here active. At the teeth the front and tip of the tongue are both employed in forming letters. The process of letter making terminates at the lips, where the remaining sounds are made.

But the sounds mentioned last were really the first, on account of the active concern of the human face in the original gesture language which afterwards became improved into language proper. Because of the use of the lips in significant gesture the first sounds were necessarily labials. The other end of our tube should, to be more complete, have attached to it a face and the mouth should be as flexible and capable of contraction and as apt in rounding the aperture as the lips of the human subject. It would then appear very natural that the first sounds used in audible language should be only those which are produced there. The making of letters once begun at the outer end of the voice tube, the manufacture of vowels and consonants would proceed in an orderly manner from without inwards. This is what has taken place in the Chinese language. There has been a labial period, a tooth period and a guttural period and these have been followed by a period of tones, representing the stage in which at presnt we meet the Chinese language in its still unfinished development. It has grown up from its root in the highest antiquity appearing first in northern and western China till, extending east and south and giving birth to many branches, it has like a vast tree spread its shade over all the eighteen provinces of the empire, and become the speech of three hundred millions of people.

In the primeval gesture language the hand would be most energetically engaged, being indispensable in obtaining food and for self defence as well as innumerable other duties and actions. The mouth requires the tongue, palate, teeth, and lips for the purposes of nutrition. Let us assume that their application as an apparatus for speech was later than their use in nutrition. Let us also assume that the use of the nose tube for ordinary respiration was anterior to its use in forming the letters *m*, *n* and *ng*. The mouth and nose being constantly occupied with their duties as the sustainers of human life, would take part also in gestures for communicating thought. The hands would be kept in ceaseless activity as the ministers of the mind during all this period. In the construction of simple implements, in all the daily activities of man, in the attempt to communicate ideas, perpetual use would be made of this member. The activity of the hand has been in the formation of words of the most far-reaching character. What the mouth has done in making letters, the hand has done in making words. As the teeth, tongue, palate, and lips were first occupied in the processes of nutrition, and afterwards in forming vowels and consonants for use in speech, so the hands first took part in the hundred manual acts necessary for the daily life of man, and then assisted in forming words and rendering them suitable to take their place in the vocabulary and grammar of language.

The outer world presents to the mind the beautiful and multitudinous objects of sense all in an orderly arrangement. The mind takes note of the limiting lines of space and time according to which every thing heavenly or earthly is disposed. The categories of the physical universe become those of the mind. The laws of language harmonize with them and are based upon them. Space and time have seemed to some philosophers to be only in the mind. But in reality space and time are in the universe and the mind sees things as they are in space and in time, and proceeds to build up the categories of logic and grammar in accordance with the observed disposition of things in the cosmos.

The mind only arrived at the realization of the ideas of grammar and logic by the help of the hand faithfully and constantly afforded during the period when language was beginning its career. Soon words would be made, and the hand would receive its name from the sound produced by its action imitated. It was then necessary to arrange the objects of thought in the memory as right and left, as before and behind, as above and below. All this was done by pointing with the hand in the first instance. At first the hand and the act of pointing would have a name common to them both. This name was applied to the categories of space as above, below, or otherwise. Either the name of the hand was applied to each location in succession and a new word made with a modification in sound to mark the idea, or some other word under the mind's permission crept in to discharge this duty. The substantive verb and the category of «is» and «is not», of «is right» and «is not right» would also originate in connection with the act of pointing with the hand. The name to be given whether affirmative or negative would as I suppose for want of another be the name of the hand as it was pronounced at the time. A modifying variation in sound would be added. That such a variation was made we have proof in such words as 受 *sheu* «receive» in the rising intonation, but heard in the even tone in the sense «give». Afterwards B. C. 300 the even tone was changed for the departing tone. So it was with 好 *hau* «good» and «to love», 買 *mai* «to buy» and «to sell». The wordmaker wanted the words «to love» and «to sell», and he formed them out of «good» and «buy» by adding an intonation existing in his environment. This took place in the tone age and in a similar way words in the guttural age would change one of their letters for a guttural. Thus when the language was in its early stages the name of the hand might be used for any act of the hand if only some convenient modification were introduced into the sound sufficing make it into a word which would be accepted by the nation. In this way the hand might be the agent in a hundred instances in bestowing names upon actions.

We need not be surprised if we shoud find that on account of the great length of time during which the language has lasted all or nearly all the auxiliary words of Chinese grammar, the causative, the passive auxiliaries, the demonstratives, the connectives of possession, the case particles, the prepositions, the adverbs *mite* of and place and many more are more or less nearly related to the hand. This idea that the name of the hand gave names to actions should not be pushed so far as to exclude sporadic roots arising adventitiously in certain circumstances from the imitation of natural sounds and through the use of metaphor, but it seems to be a good working hypothesis that in a very large number of cases the hand was the source of the name and that most roots are derivatives from the name of the hand.

The main reason for this hypothesis is that there is no way of accounting for roots so well. The action of the hand produced some sound of collision, or reverberation which made a name for the hand possible. But when this had been established in use it was easier to form the name of other actions by derivation from this established name than to make an entirely new name. This greater ease of formation would give an advantage to such a derivative over other possible roots formed by imitating *de novo* some natural sound.

Whenever the hand proved insufficient as a base on which to build up new words, the natural sounds attendant on so many actions would supply the deficiency.

The historical instance above given of words newly formed with the help of a tone, attached to some old word, is important as showing, by what has taken place in the period when a new intonation was growing into prevalence, the effect of a new environment. The word maker adopts what the new environment affords. So by analogy before the time of historical records there would be a period when guttural letters became a fashion. Palatal letters, sibilants, tooth letters, nasals each had a time of popularity, and at any particular epoch when new words had to be made and discriminated by a sound, that particular initial or final which was then popular would naturally take its place in the new word. Further the popularity of certain letters must have occurred in a certain succession. Only one or two letters can be new favourites at one and the same time. Tones have come into use in a fixed succession as is known. So it has been with letters. There could not have been at any one time more than a certain limited strain on the language-making faculties. This renders it inevitable that as there was a labial age at first with *p*, *b*, *m* and the vowels *a*, *o*, *i*, so the other letters whether vowels or consonants must have been developed in a succession which careful investigation may bring to light. Language like a tree springs from a simple beginning and its stem and branches take a long time to grow before flowers and fruit appear.

II.

FIRST EFFORTS AT IMITATION OF NATURAL SOUNDS BY THE HUMAN MOUTH EXEMPLIFIED IN THE CHINESE LANGUAGE.

Any natural sound produced by human action or heard by the human ear might form materials for the first words. But the sounds heard are usually too rough and too undefined to become current words such as would be symbols of clear ideas. For instance the crack of a hammer or club not coming from a tube is a more or less confused noise unsuitable for easy imitation by the voice. It needs to be hewn, and polished like a stone fresh from the quarry, before it can enter the temple of human language. This process of special manipulation and preparation to which sounds are subjected to fit them to become words, is, under the direction of the thinking faculty in man, the work of the vocal organs.

The sound receives its meaning from the human imagination and its place in the vocabulary and in grammar is assigned it by the logical faculty. The special form it takes is given to it by the tongue, teeth, lips, nose and other organs. The voice produces the first rough representative of the natural sound. It is in the larynx above the wind pipe that the initial operations connected with the sounds of language are conducted. The air comes from the lungs pushed on by the muscular action of that region. The vocal cords which bound the glottis at the top of the windpipe are set vibrating, and the vibrations make the voice. The voice takes its particular form in the mouth and nose. It there becomes speech, its elements being vowels and consonants and its complete shape the word as it appears in language.

The first wordmakers began with labial letters because these are more open to observation by the eye than the others. When *p, b, m* are pronounced, the action of the lips is seen. Throat letters like *k* and *g* would naturally come into current use after labials, because the action of the back of the tongue in closing the sound passage is not visible. By similar reasoning it may be expected that letters formed by the front and tip of the tongue would come into use later than the labials and earlier than the throat letters. Father in old Chinese is *ba* and mother *ma* (1). The interest felt by parents in teaching their children many things would powerfully aid in developing primitive language. To some extent the sounds first learned by children may be taken to be an index to the sounds first used by man in primitive language, the first rude forms of speech.

The priority of labial letters over other consonants is rendered probable by the facts of letter change in China. As a rule the order observable in the changes of letters whether initial or final is from lips to throat or from lips to teeth or from teeth to throat, but not from teeth and throat to the lips. Thus, *p* produces *f* or *h*, but *f* and *h* do not change to *p* (2). There are exceptions, but this is the general rule.

(1) We obtain these sounds from the rhymes of the Book of Odes when judged of by the help of the transcription of Sanscrit words at Loyang A. D. 67 and in the II nd Century.

(2) For other examples see my Study of the Chinese Characters pp. 181 to 211.

In the natural order of linguistic development we see in the first stages of language much of gesture, of which the action of the lips is a part. Afterwards gesture ceases when language by attaining greater variety and complexity in its sounds also becomes more efficient. Men then abandon gesture in order not to spend more energy than the occasion requires. This first period when lip letters were much in use and other letters of rare occurrence and when there was the incessant employment of various gestures caused by the action of the hands, face and other parts of the body, may be called from the preponderance of labial letters at that time the labial period.

Evidence of the continuous decline of the labials in language may be found in Chinese. Thus in modern dictionaries the initial letters m, p, f occupy a space only half of that occupied by h and k and ng, and not much more than one fourth of the space occupied by words commencing with t, s, n, j, ch. Since the front and point of the tongue are both engaged in forming the initials t, s, n, j, ch, we may divide the words in this case into two great groups. Each of them has nearly twice as many words as the labial initials. So in the use of the finals k, t, p which had existed in the language till the seventh century, there were then as the Dictionary Kwang-yün shows, twice as many words with final t as with final p, and three times as many with final k as with final p. Words with final m were as 32, while n and ng were as 84 and 80 respectively, that is to say words with final m were scarely one third as many as words with n or ng. Thus 1200 years ago the lip letters p, b, m, had lost a great part of their share in the Chinese vocabulary and since that time they have lost much more. Hence it may be concluded that there has been an immense migration of letters which has destroyed the predominance of labials existing in the first period of the Chinese language and that it was by change of *p* to *t* and *k* and of *m* to *n* and *ng* that the tongue and throat letters have obtained their present great prevalence in the vocabulary. Roots at that early time would be chiefly labial, and when dental, lingual and guttural roots appeared, it was probably more often by letter change than new creation. The age of labials was also the age of gesture and it is in the light of necessity that this question of the priority of labial letters must be regarded. The sight of opening and closing lips is in the first stage of language an aid to intelligibility. The speaker must see in order both to understand and to imitate. The labials are the easiest letters to pronounce.

The time during which there was the greatest predominance of *p*, *b*, *m* in Chinese roots, was before the formation of the characters, assigned by tradition to about B. C. 2500. For in the phonetic characters the six final consonants *p*, *t*, *k*, *m*, *n*, *ng* are neither of them wanting. Examining the phonetic characters we find that as a rule final *p*, occurring in any phonetic, belongs to all words written with the same phonetic. It follows then that final *p* was certainly in the pronunciation of the inventors of the character. The same is true of the other five final consonants found in Chinese words.

We are thus made to some extent aware of the wide range in time over whih changes in the Chinese language extend. It is still a living language spoken by more individuals than any other language in the world, and it is after more than four thousand years still passing through letter changes under the eyes of the student. It is possible by means of the phonetic element in the structure of the language to trace laws of change up to B. C. 2500 and then farther back by the careful comparison of the words in their relation to each other.

Since the Chinese language was already a medium in which eighteen hundred (1) years before Mencius there were written records to preserse the data of astronomy, the facts of history, and the interpretations of the diviner, we may expect that the letters were at that time fairly well developed.

1. There would be the nasals *m, n, ng*. These would have the priority because the nose tube is usually open for respiration and it remains open while these letters are pronounced. The letters *b, g*, and *d* agree with these letters in regard to closing the mouth barriers but differ in requiring the nose channel to be shut. There is therefore more difficulty in pronouncing *b, g* and *d*, and this would naturally give to *m, n*, and *ng* the first place.

2. Coming to *b, d* and *g* with *p, t, k*, the voiced and unvoiced checks which belong to the three mouth barriers we ask which are the older. There is a reason for regarding *b, d, g* as the older. In the modern language *p, t, k*, have been evolved fron them. This happened when *b d* and *g* were abandoned by the mandarin dialect. It is probable that it was by a like process at some ancient date that the old *p, t* and *k* took the place of *b, d* and *g*. We cannot tell when this was because the rhymes of poetry do not help us here. Another reason for assigning priority to *b, d, g* is that they are more audible and in primitive times this advantage would be of no little value. Also Manchu and Mongol have *b, d, g* and not *p, t, k*.

3. The analogy of Manchu and Mongol would lead to the supposition that the aspirated *p, t, k*, were early introduced among Chinee current sounds. They were found useful for marking special meanings, for emphasis and for insuring great distinctness. In Sanscrit they exist, but as compared with the pure *p, t, k*, the

(1) Mencius (last chapter) makes Yau to have lived about 1850 years before his time i. e. B. C. 2150. Mencius died 13 C 289,

words in which they occur are only as two or three in a hundred. Apirated consonants in fact occur in high and windy latitudes where conversation is loud and needs to be very distinct in order to be well understood. In Chinese they occur as a device rather to multiply syllables in a monosyllabic language. Where the variety attained by the polysyllable is wanting the monosyllabic stem must be stretched and strained in every possible way in order to find forms to symbolize the ever increasing number of new terms. In the oldest Chinese records words read with the unaspirated p, t, k are to the aspirated as three to one in the very old Yau-tien, and as two to one in the sixty four names of the combinations in the Yi-ching, the much revered diviner's Manual and first among the classics.

4. There would probably also be in existence B. C. 2500 s, r, sh, zh, the mixed consonants of Mr. Melville Bell's system called so because the front and point of the tongue are in use at the same time to form these letters. The letter s being very audible and distinct would come early into currency. The reason why it has so clear a sound is that the point of the tongue approaches the upper gum, and the front of the tongue nearly touches the palatal arch. It appears in Chinese not seldom as a modification of t. So sh, in which the tongue has much the same configuration except that the tongue's point is farther from the gum and the front of the tongue only approaches the outer rim of the palatal arch, is also along with the compound ch, a modification of t. Thus 心 *sim* heart is *tim* in Cochin Chinese, because that is a very old dialect of the Chinese language and preserves many ancient sounds. In Chinese evolution the letters s and sh both proceed from t. In B. C. 2500 consequently fewer words would begin with s and sh than at present.

5. In regard to *w* and *y* with their aspirates *hw*, *hy* they are probably letters of an origin later than the primitive age. *Y* is chiefly a substitute for *d*, *t* or *ng* which once existed in its place. *W* is a substitute for *m* or *ng*. They need not then be primitive. *Y* and *W* are in close relation to *i* and *u*. In the letter *y* we have voice with the front of the tongue contracting the passage between it and the roof of the mouth. *I* has the same configuration but the channel is less contracted and shorter. The aspirate precedes the configuration of *y* for *hy*. In *w* the lower lip and back of the tongue contract the oral passage at the same time that the voice passes. In *hw* the aspirate precedes.

The letters *f*, *v*, *l*, *r* are not likely to have had a very early origin. *F* and *v* are formed by the lower lip touching the upper teeth in the middle of the oral passage. To add voice is to change *f* to *v*. If the point of the tongue be turned inward and the lower surface of the same organ come close to the front wall of the palate, a rush of voice passing at the same moment makes *l*. These three letters are in Chinese substitutes for *p*, *b* and *d* and are not to be supposed to be primitive. The Chinese *r* is heard when the tip of the tongue is turned back and the under surface of the same organ is brought to the front wall of the palate. It is a modern substitute for *ni*. A glide with voice precedes *r* and no vowel follows it, so that it is properly written *er*. When a vowel follows *er* becomes *zh*. The Pekinese do not as a rule curl the end of the tongue when pronouncing it and the sound is then simply the ninth glide in Mr. Melville Bell's arrangement.

6. The vowels *a*, *i*, *o* would naturally be the oldest of all vowels. There is a wider opening of the mouth for *a* than for the other two. The letter *a* then would be aided in obtaining currency by its superior visibility. So *o* would be aided by its roundness

and *i* by the narrowness of the aperture. These primitive vowels were followed by *u*, *ü* which are less visible from without and would be later. There are other Chinese vowels found in 旦 *tan*, 丁 *ting*, 更 *keng*, 舍 *she*, 角 *chio*. All these vowels may have been formed from *a* by tendency to variation. The modern Chinese *o* represents the ancient *a*. The *i* of old Chinese as formed by the convex front of the tongue advancing to very near the palatal arch is after *s*, *sh*, *ch*, in modern Chinese exchanged for a peculiar vowel *ï* formed by narrowing the orifice between the tongue and palate. The older *o* and *ü* have both become *u*. So it is with other vowels. The old have changed into the new. The lesson taught by studying the ancient sounds and the dialects is that the farther we go back the nearer we approach to unity. As the consonants are reduced to labials in the first instance, so the vowels are reduced to *a* which would be the first to obtain currency because it is most observable by the eye.

III.

GROUPING OF THE LETTERS.

The tongue of any one speaking is from time to time moved upward to contract or shut the sound passage. The lower lip moves upward also. This makes a fourfold division, that is to say we have gutturals, palatals, dentals and labials. The upper lip and teeth with the palate are at rest. The lower lip, and teeth with the tip, front and back of the tongue are always kept moving. The air coming from the lungs may be a breathing or a voice. In either case there is the formation of a letter in Chinese. The breathing is *h* which may be high or low, the high breathing being caused by increased quickness in vibration in the sound passage at the back of the tongue. With voice the letters formed may be *b, d, g, z, zh, m* etc. The vowels are also in two series. The upper and lower *a, i, o* when initial are all distinguished in old native dictionaries.

The upward movement of the tongue at its three points of departure, the back, front, or point, may contract, divide, or close up the sound passage and may contract it more or less. To close the passage at back, teeth or lips, is to make *k, t, p*. To divide it in the middle at the upper gum is to make *l*. To contract the sound passage in a very slight degree is to produce vowels. If we make the passage very small, we pronounce consonants. In a midway position we have what Mr. Bell calls glides. There are in all thirty six vowels, twelve glides and about eighty consonants. Among these the lip letters, nasals and throat letters are included with those formed by the tongue. Less than half of these are in use among the Chinese.

The waves of vocal air on arriving at the soft palate either pass along the nose tube, or the mouth tube, or both. In the nose tube there are no modifications of the sound at least in Chinese (1). In the mouth channel the modifications are those of a flexible tube liable to contraction and expansion at every point of the journey to the lips. The soft palate marks the division into nasals and non-nasals.

Among the vowels *W* and *Y* become consonants when they begin a word. But this is not all. They are employed when preceded by *k, h, s, ch, p, t, m, n, l* to form compound initials. Thus we have formed with *w* such syllables as *kwan, kwei, hwan, hwei, shwen, chwen, twan, lwan*. Among these the last *loan* is rather an instance of a true diphthong, the sound of *o* being distinct. We have with *y* such syllables as *chiuen, hsiuen, sie, pye, tye, mye, nye, lye*. In 年, 眼 *nien* "year", *yien* "eye" we have a clearly sounded *i*

(1) There are however nasals in Amoy.

followed by *e*. But most of such syllables have *y* and this letter and *w* may be viewed as consonants just as we have *s* and *sh* helping to make up the compound consonants *ts* and *tsh*. The reason that *u* and *i* only among the vowels can become consonants is that they contract the sound passage more than other vowels.

The aspirate precedes *w*, *y*, and *s* with the vowels. It follows *k*, *t*, and *p*, which close the passage. We should write 會 *hwei* and not *hui* because the *w* is here a consonant. So we should spell 玄, 全 *hsyuen* "dark", *'chyuen* "the whole", if we would be consistent and exact, because *y* is here a consonant. In *hs* the process is as follows; the breath that forms the aspirate having escaped finds the sound tube contracted into the narrow shape required to produce the sound *s*. This contraction begins at the middle of the roof of the mouth and continues to the rim of the palate. A shrill sibilation passes along on the right and left of the tongue the middle of which is raised longitudinally so as to be higher than the sides. The compound initial *hs* before the vowels *i*, *ü* has come out of *hi*, *hü*, *si*, *sü*, sounds which formerly existed, and which still exist in Nanking Mandarin. It is the narrowness of the tube caused by the configuration of the vowel *i* and consonant *y* and of the letter *s* that causes this peculiar sound. The configuration of *s* remains but more breath passes. The aspirated *k*, *t*, *p*, are simply the union of two letters in each case. The object of this is to increase the resources of a limited syllabary. *Kai* "ought" is distinguished in this way from *khai* " to open. " ,

The sibilants *s* and *sh* are the most suitable letters to make compounds with *t*. These compounds originated in a simple *t*. There was an insertion of *s* and *sh* at different periods to make more variety in the syllabary. The monosyllabism of the language forces the two consonants into the closest proximity. They coalesce so accurately that they become undivided to the ear. This is specially true of *t* and *sh* which become *ch*. The closeness of the union brings the upper and lower teeth together. In old Chinese there was no general change of *k* to *ch*. But this phenomenon has now appeared in north and west China. When *k* precedes *i* or *ü* it becomes *ch*. That is to say the tongue closes the voice passage not at the back but in front. It does so because the vowels which follow require the front of the tongue to be drawn up and there will consequently be a saving of exertion by omitting the check at the back.

Among all the Chinese letters, *h*, *w*, *y*, *s*, and *sh* are the only consonants that follow an initial. The insertion of *l* and *r* is common in other languages. Not so in Chinese. The *h* inserted as an aspirate appears to have been needed to intensify a shade of meaning. *W* and *y* have been inserted from an endogenous tendency to widen the pith of the word stem. Thus *chiang* " a river " 江 comes from *kong*. *Shwang* " a pair " comes from *shong*. Further the letters *s* and *sh* are both insertions and have no connection with the root. The initial *t* which they follow is radical and so is the final which they precede. The cause of these insertions was that more syllables came to be needed.

Vowels may be grouped as belonging to the back or front of the tongue. *A*, *o*, *u* and short *u* (*u* in *sun*) are back vowels and are in old Chinese fond of *k*(1) as a final. The vowels *i*, *e* (in *men*), *ü*, *ö* are front vowels and are fond in old Chinese of *p* or *t* as a final. If the *a* in 山 *shan* " mountain " and 商 *shang* " merchant " be compared they will be found to differ. The *a* of *shang* has a larger

---

(1) As in Shanghai where vowels pronounced chiefly with the back of the tongue prefer final *k*. Those which require the aid of the lips and teeth have there no final consonant.

oral cavity and prefers *ng* while the less expanded *a* of 山 *shan* prefers the nasal *n*. If we divide the vowels into groups according to their natural relationship we may obtain light on the old consonant finals. Thus in Peking the diphthong *iau* 學 *hiau* " learn " is an index to the lost final *k*. This diphthong does not occur in words whose final was *t* or *p*.

The vowels may be divided into rounded and not rounded. The rounded are *a*, *u* (in *sun*, *run*), *i*, *à* (in *man*). The rounding takes place *all along* the voice cavity, and becomes visible at the lips.

Mr. Melville Bell also divides vowels into primary and wide. The vowels in 依 *i*, 舍 *she*, 分 *fen*, are primary. The vowels in 他 *t'a*, 山 *shan*, 新 *hsin*, are examples of wide vowels. The vowels in 都, 多 *tu*, *to* are primary while *u* in 東 *tung* is wide. Wide quality is occasioned by the expansion of the pharynx and the drawing back of the soft palate. In Shanghai the wide vowels belong to the short tone in most instances.

The causes of variation in letters may be noticed quite plainly in some cases. When it is said that back vowels such as *a*, *o*, *u* and some others are fond of *k*, it means that the muscular contraction producing *k* affects the size of the oral cavity. When final *p* changes to final *k* the tongue moves down by sympathy, widens the cavity and produces some one of the back vowels.

So also a change from final *p* to final *t* would tend to produce high vowels by the rising of the tongue when it forms *t*.

Afterwards when *p*, *t*, and *k*, were all dropped, the tongue not requiring to make the checks *t* and *k*, would naturally sink and there would appear a predominance of *a*, *o*, and *u*. It would then be easy for *w* and *y* to slip in just after the initial. Thus *kak* would become *chiau*, or *kau*.

A variation in vowels would be produced by the change of final *m* to *n* and to *ng*. The letter *n* requires the tongue tip to move up. This would cause the preceding vowel to narrow its cavity. The letter *ng* replacing *m* would occasion an expansion of the vowel cavity and open the way in consequence for new vowels and diphthongs having their location in the neighbourhood of the soft palate. The reason why we have *pen* " root" for the old *pun* is that *e* (*io* in *nation)* is a back vowel like *u (oo* in *good)*.

The cause of the migration of letters from without inwards is economy of energy or change of muscular action. The change from *g* and *k* to *h*, as in *gau* or *kau* "thick" to *heu*, saves the pressure of the tongue against the soft palate. The change of *b*, *d* and *g*, to *p*, *t*, *k* saves the puff of voice which sonant letters require. These little economies are not however allowed by the presiding mind until there is a guarantee that the intelligibility of speech will not be diminished. There are compensations also in many ways. The new language for instance often uses two words where one would suffice. In the old language the orthoepy was distinct and the style laconic. In modern speech words are often clipped and incomplete, but there is more expansiveness of phrase to balance this loss.

The cause of variability is economy of energy, or rest from muscular contraction in one spot, or the effort of the mind to increase the powers of the syllabary and then make new words. Advance in industry and civilization demanded new words. and this is the way in which the demand was met.

Another distinct cause of change in some consonants is the narrowing of the oral cavity when the vowels *i. ü* are pronounced. The effect of this narrowing is that *ts* and *k* both become *ch*. The raising of the front of the tongue towards the front of the palatal arch to make *i* and *ü* is anticipated and *sh* is the result. In other words *sh* is akin to *i* and *ü* and becomes inserted before them and after the initial *k* or *t*. *Tsing* "quiet" and *king* "to honour" both become *ching*. *S* after *t* becomes *sh* in these circumstances.

The vocal variations employed by the human will to modify monosyllabic words may be stated as aspirating, nasalizing, sibilization, lingualization, insertion of vowels and of *l* and *r* after an initial, prefix of *s* before *p*, *t*, or *k*, insertion of *s* after *p*, *t*, *k*, lengthening and shortening vowels. In Chinese *t* changes to *s* and takes *s* after it, but it is not so with *p* and *k*. Yet *k* changes to *tsh*. While Spanish and Japanese change *f* to *h*, Chinese prefers to change *k* to *h*. Chinese never inserts *r* or *l* after an initial check.

IV

DEVELOPMENT OF TONES AND OF THE UPPER AND LOWER SERIES OF VOWELS AND CONSONANTS.

The voice is originated at the top of the wind pipe by the passage of air through the glottis causing the vocal cords to vibrate. The vibration is communicated by the air as it passes out of the glottis through the mouth and nostrils as a sound differing in quality in individuals. The vocal cords have great variety of length and tension. They are narrow bands two in number which are about one third shorter in women than in men. The tones and pitch in the human voice are regulated by the muscular action brought to bear on these cords and on the air which passes between them.

The pronunciation of Chinese is marked by a double pitch and by simple or compound inflexions of tone. All features of this kind constituting tone and pitch, with loudness and quality of the voice are imparted to the vocal breath, while still in the larynx. Thus every word in fact receives its upward or downward inflexion or its monotone effect before it comes under the shaping influence which originates vowels and consonants. But on account of the brief time taken up by the passage of the air and the action of the nerves and muscles on the various organs employed in speech, this priority in utterance of tone as compared with vowels and consonants is not perceived by the ear of the listener.

We have in China the upper and lower series of letters and tones in the old middle dialect, and of tones only in Fukien and Canton. These are separated by an interval of a second in city dialects and by a wider interval in country places where enunciation is more emphatic. This means not a widening and contracting of the sound channel, for pitch and tone have nothing to do with this. It means simply a difference in the rapidity and slowness of the vibrations in the vocal cords and in the air which passes through them.

This double pitch sometimes becomes triple when a particular intonation is set very low whether as monotone or inflection.

The question when the upper and lower series commenced is historically very much the same with the question when the distinction between voiced and unvoiced consonants or sonants and surds began. It is necessary to bear in mind that the difference between voiced and unvoiced does not affect the quality of a vowel. In the Tang dynasty the difference in pitch which we now find uniformly maintained from Shanghai to Canton must have certainly existed, and we may assume that it existed long before that time, the mandarin pronunciation in which the sonants have disappeared being then entirely unknown. The surds present all the appearance of having been intruders. For example 京 *king* in the old Geography 山海經 *Shan-hai-king* and some other early authorities is pronounced *ging* or *giang*, The word 街 *chieh, kiai,* "street" is but the changed form of 衢 *c'hü, gü,* "highway." The evolution here taking place is that of *g* to *k*.

The word 陽 *yang*, *dom* "light" is the original from which 昌 *c'hang*, *t'am*, is derived. For very many surd initials a corresponding sonant is easily found. The sonant has been the mother form from which the surd has been evolved. We see this in mandarin where what were once sonants are all now surds. Hence the sonants being primitive and the surds derived we may conclude there was in the primitive state of the language no difference of pitch in pronouncing the initial consonants. When the surds were evolved the double pitch would be originated at the same time in order to give them more distinctness.

The tones include rising and falling inflections and monotones. In the fifth century after Christ there were but four. They were called from their quality even, rising, departing, entering. This was several centuries before mandarin was in existence. In choosing names for the four tones the makers of the first tables of sounds selected the words even, rising, departing and entering because these words exemplified the tones of which they were the names. The even tone was a monotone without inflection. The rising tone was a rising inflection. The departing tone would have been called the 下 *hia sheng* or the 落 *lok sheng* in the sense "falling", but this would not have been fitting because *hia* was in the rising tone and *lok* in the entering tone. The tone called *ju sheng* by the makers of the early sound tables was heard as it is at present in south China with the catch of which Mr. Melville Bell speaks as a depression of the epiglottis such as any one may observe when in the act of swallowing. This is precisely what the Chinese use as the entering or short tone, when *k, t, p,* are not pronounced as at Shanghai where *p* and *t* as finals are no longer heard. The epiglottis closes the glottis and this is indicated by final *h* in the dictionaries of Morrison, Medhurst, and Williams.

In the Odes of B. C. 800 there are three tones, but in the poetry of the Han dynasty there are four. Thus we learn that tones are of gradual introduction. Language began without them. In the Chinese development of language it was the nasals, sonants, and vowels that were most important. At first tones were not needed, they came in when final letters began to be dropped. This we learn from the fact that it was only in words with vowel endings that the rising tone was at first used. All the words ending in *m, n, ng*, were then heard in the even tone and this state of things continued down to the time of the poet Ch'ŭ-yuen, about B. C. 300. If we consult Twan-yŭ-ts'ai's tables we find that 壽 *sheu* "otd age", 就 *tsieu* "approach", were with 道 *do* "way, doctrine", heard in the rising tone. But 共 *gong* "together", 送 *song* "to escort", were in the even tone. Before the Odes were written, if we judge by the evidence before us, no single word ending with *ng, n* or *m*, had left the even tone. The same is true down to the time when the departing tone with vowel finals first appeared. In the Han poetry departing tone words with vowel finals began early to rhyme with each other. The Tai-yuen-king of Yang-hiufang shews this and also the collection in six volumes of Han and Wei poetry published in the 17th century by Mei-ling-tsu. In the same work words now in the rising and departing tone with consonant finals are all found rhyming with words in the rising and even tone respectively. Should the curious inquirer examine these volumes, he will find 世 *shi*, 路 *lu* in the departing tone and 欵, 患 *t'an, hwan*, in the even tone. From this fact we learn that just as in the previous age when the rising tone was forming the vowel finals moved first to be followed subsequently in the Han dynasty by the consonants, so it was with the departing tone. First in the Han dynasty the vowel finals moved and after the age of the Three kingdoms, A. D. 300, the consonant finals followed. Thus it was that in the 5th century when the discovery of the tones was made, the number was stated to be four. The poetry of the Three kingdoms enables us to decide that the deporting tone, Sir Th. Wade's 4th tone, was not completed till the 4th century.

The four tones remained undisturbed from the fifth century till about the 11th when the even tone on account of the change from sonant to surd which then took place was divided into two parts, the 1st and 2nd tones of Sir Th. Wade. Intonation began to play the part which had hitherto been played by surd and sonant. China became weary of sonants and abandoned them for ever. Aspirates and surds took their place and they were pronounced in a new tone. The additonal muscular force which makes voice was exchanged for that which produced an intonation. A little later the entering tone lost its finals k, t, and p. They do not appear in the Baschpa transcription made in Marco Polo's time. The cause was that the muscular force required to close the mouth barriers was felt to be too great an exertion. The brigade of words which belonged to this tone became scattered, some joining one of the new tones and some another. This was a relief to the tone-forming muscles in the walls of the larynx which objected to the extra work caused by the bisection of the even tone.

The successive origination of the tones is historically proved. Their growth can be measured by centuries; they have taken the place of the alphabet as aids to the mind in forming words, and they may be compared to new forests of timber growing over coal beds whose vegetation was quite of another sort and tells of a very different climate from that which nourishes the forests of to-day.

Since it is indubitable that the tones are evolved one from another in the later development of the language it is to be expected that the various groups of letters in the earlier age before the invention of writing would also be evolved one out of the other. There is in language a development resembling the gradual and uniform change claimed for the rocks of the earth by the best geologists. Lip letters slowly became tooth letters and sibilants and gutturals till the alphabet was complete.

The origin of the Chinese tones is to be sought in the restrictions of the syllabary and vocabulary, and in the convenience found in m:king use of intonations to express opposite meanings or variations in sense. Thus, 機 *ki*, with the meant "fulcrum", "pivot", "centre of motion", "source" even tone. When the word 幾 *ki* "how many" was formed it took the rising tone, and was written with 幾 because it had a surd initial, but was distinguished from it by the new intonation then originating. Anciently the left hand appendage, the wood radical, would not be used. A Chinese hinge is an upright pivot on which the post of a door revolves. The same word is a table or stool small in size. It may be derived from a verb of cutting and compared with the particle *ko* in *che-ko* 這箇 "this", and with the pronoun 其 *k'i*, *c'hi* "that".

The slow growth of the Chinese tone system and its tendency to subdivision in localities are very marked. Slow growth is in favour of a uniformitarian theory of development for the Chinese language. The fact that such a peculiarity as the tone system is not primeval but has grown up by gradual change is also in favour of the theory that at an early stage the Chinese language was one with the other Asiatic languages.

Lastly, the reason why the tone age came after the age of the lip and tooth letters was because change began at the lips, advanced inward over the tongue, and at length reached the throat, the proper seat of tones, of the aspirate, and of the upper and lower pitch of the voice.

There is an analogy between the late use of tones in Chinese and their late introduction into European speech. The use of the upper rising inflection for questions in European languages is a case in point. This interrogative inflection has pushed out the interrogative particles to a large extent and taken their place. We can ask questions in modern speech without special particles because we have this inflection. Greek and Latin were much more plentifully supplied than we are with interrogative particles.

Also in English we make nouns out of verbs by varying the syllabic accent. We form *cónvict* out of *convíct*, *cóncert* out of *concért*, *cónvert* out of *convért*. This was not the case in Greek and Latin. In those languages syllables specially appended discharged this duty.

In the Greek language the prevalence of tones was a very peculiar and deeply marked characteristic. As in Chinese tones followed the alphabetic development and took the place to some extent of various old forms which are found some of them in Homer. When Aristophanes of Byzantium marked the Greek accents B. C. 200, he professed to follow Attic models. As to the age when tones entered the Greek language we are in ignorance. All we know is that Attic speech paid great attention to the tones. There was time enough between the age of Homer and B. C. 200 for considerable changes to take place in tones, but what those changes were we cannot tell.

There can be no doubt that in Cicero's time the interrogative force was marked by inflection. He says of Catiline : " Hic tamen vivit. Vivit? immo vero etiam in Senatum venit." The first *"vivit"* has the inflection of the indicative which would be either even or quick falling. The second *"vivit"* necessarily has the rising or interrogative inflection and it must have been uttered with great vivacity to open the way for the sentence following: "he comes even into the Senate." In this sentence the chief accent is on the middle syllable of *Senatum* and the verb *venit* at the end is lightly pronounced. It is by the influence of Turanian grammar that the verb occurs at the end of the sentence.

The time when sonants became surds was probably early in the tone period. Surd initials are common in the oldest parts of the Book of History. *Tsang* "to bury", *t'ien* "heaven", and the like are not very primitive looking. *Tsang* is derived from "to hide". *T'ien* is that which is spread out. If they originated in the dental period as is possible, the surds may be conjectured to have branched off from the sonants at that time.

V.

In the Chinese syllables in the old language vowel endings are rare. It is better to regard a closed syllable as the type of a Chinese word. Originally the sound might be *bam, ba* or *ab; am, ma,* or *mam. I* and *o* taking the place of *a* would increase the number of primeval syllables to eighteen. Probability is in favour of *m* over *b.* In primitive gesture language the act of closing the lips after the vowel *a* is very likely to have been in use as a significant action. To close the lips and then pronounce the vowel would be a more complex action. We may therefore assume that *am* and *ab* preceded *ma* and *ba.*

But passing over that period in the evolution of language when *ab* may have preceded *ba,* it will be well to recognize that a syllable closed at both ends is more suitable to the genius of the Chinese word.

The hand strikes an object. A noise of collision is heard. By the tendency to imitation the mind strives to reproduce the sound and operates on the mouth through the nerves. The most susceptible part is the lips. In pronouncing *bam* there is an act of closing the lips first. The soft palate closes the nose passage. The sound *b* is then heard. *A* follows it and *m* at the end, involving an act of opening the lips, and then closing them. Considering the facility felt in using the lips, there can be but one opinion as to the probability that they were used in forming letters before the other vocal organs.

Let us ask what we have in this word *bam* for the noise of collision. It commences and ends with a letter which is in both cases visible to the eye by the action of the lips. The vowel *a* also is made exceptionally visible by the opening of the lips as we pronounce that letter. Two hard objects meet violently. The sound is not exactly *bam,* but we make it so by an adroit use of our lips, thus improving upon the first rough imitation. After successive efforts to reproduce the sound, some one form obtains currency in a small community. Let it be *bam.*

We find in Chinese that *b* may become *p* or *f* or *p* aspirated, or *m.* We very frequently find roots which agree in meaning and differ only in initial as *bang, dang, gang,* and of these there are so many examples that they suggest a law. The only reasonable explanation is that interchange in the initial has caused this phenomenon.

As examples let the following be considered : 幫 *pang,* 相 *siang,* 匡 *k'wang* "assist, be at the side of any one, aid". The verb "to lift up" is expressed by 拔 *bat*, 提 *di*, 舉 *chü, kü*. "Form of a thing" is expressed by 範 *fan, bam*, 狀 *chwang, dong*, 形 *hsing, hing*. Frozen and hard substances are 冰 *ping* "ice", 凌 *ling* "ice", 剛 *kang* "steel". "To wind rope, or other objects", is 盤 *p'an, ban*, 纏 *c'han, dan*, 拴 *shwen* "bind up", 捲 *chiuen, kiuen* "roll up". The adverbs for "enough, satisfied", 飽 *pau, pok* "satisfied", 足 *tsu, tsok* "enough", 彀 *keu, kok* "enough". "Knives" are 砭 *pien, pim* "stone, lancet", 鍼 *chen, tim* "lancet, needle", 劍 *chien, kim* "sword". "Prosperous" is *feng, sheng* or *hing*. "All" is 普 *p'u*, 都 *tu* or 皆 *kiai, chieh*. "To seek " is 覓 *mik* 索 *sok*, 求 *qieu, c'hieu, gok*. "A jar" is *p'ing, ying* or *kang*.

Examples are so numerous that the best hypothesis appears to be that the initial has changed from labial to dental or guttural. This is more probable than that separate roots were created. Usually this leap from labial to dental and guttural took place before the invention of the characters. But in some instances we may observe in phonetic characters the proof of transition after the invention of writing from dental to guttural initial, For example 京 *ching, king* is *liang* in 涼 and its old sound was probably *dang* from which *liang* (1) would be evolved. The characters began to come into use before this transition of initials was completed and so the sounds of some phonetic characters begin with *g*, or with *k* in some words and with *l* in others

In modern Chinese *m* as a final has been replaced by *ng* and by *n*. There is no lack then of recent evidence of this transition. If there were need of ancient proof of transition of this kind,

---

(1) In the 1st century Yang-hiung used 京 for the sound *giang*, and the wha'o was called *giang* because it was long 長 *chang*, from which *giang* would be derived.

we have it in characters like 風 which has the old value *bam* and the new value *feng*. It is formed from 凡 *bam* "all", and in the odes it rhymed with final *m*, and ranked as having that final. This was about B. C. 800.

Thus there appears to be great flexibility in some Chinese words. Let us follow our example *bam* "to strike", into some of its derivatives. 磅 *p'ang, bem* "to meet, strike together", an intransitive verb. 逢 feng, bong "to meet", 磅 *p'ang* "sound of stones falling". an intransitive verb. So 滂 is "the roar of water", or 霶 "of a storm of snow in winter". In this case *p'ang* is the noise of the wind. 崩 *peng* "fall of a mountain", 砰 *p'eng* "fall of a rock". Such a word as 風 *feng* "wind", may be the imitation of the roaring blast or of objects falling through the violence of the wind. The word is one; the natural sounds it represents are various. Such a word as 冰 *ping* "ice" may have been named, while the final was still *m*, from the noise of collision heard either when objects fall on ice, or when ice is broken. "A staff" is 棒 *pang*. The "bee" is 蜂 *feng* and this name must be thought of as *bam* like the others, and as in other cases must be assumed to be derived from the most obvious natural sound. This will of course be the hum of the bee. But it may also be viewed as the noise of collision heard when this and similar insects strike against hard objects.

There are several derivatives beginning with *ch* and *t*. *Ch* is changed from *t* as *t* is from *p*. 撞 *chwang* "strike against an object", 創 *c'hwang* "to wound", 創 "to begin". This word is used of the agent in commencing any work or when the first sod is dug or a new era begun. We have initial *t* in 打 *ta, tang* "to beat" 璫 *tang* "ear pendents". Objects when hanging come into collision. The resulting sound furnishes a name for the act of swaying to and fro. "To obstruct the way" is named 當 *tang* from the noise of collision. "A small gong beaten by pedlars" is 鐺 *tang*, 踢 *t'ang* is "to slip down, fall or lie down", from the noise heard.

If we examine words with *k* or *h* as initials and having meanings that shew them to be derived from a root " to beat ", they are not few in number. " A hanging stone " or "bronze plate used as a musical instrument" is called 磬 *ch'ing*, *k'ing*. Any thing hanging across the way is *hwang-tsi* 幌子. "Across" is *heng*. "Across the ages" in the sense "constant", is *heng* 恒. "He who crosses the path of reason and acts wildly" is *hwang-tang*. Such words may be referred to the sense "obstruct" as their source. If *ping* "ice" is derived from the noise of collision, so 强 *ch'iang*, *giang*, 郎 *lang* " hardy ", " strong ", 硬 *ying*, *ngang* " hard " may originate in the same way. 抗 *k'ang* " resist ", is the same word as 當 *tang* " oppose " and 碰 *p'eng*, *bang* "strike against". If we meet with final *m*, it is the same thing. With the aspirated *k* as initial we find 砍 *k'am* " to strike, to stone ". 轗 *k'am* " to impede ", 戡 *k'am* "to stab, kill". Just as 當 *tang* "oppose" is also *tang* "to bear, support", so 揕 *k'am* is also "support, sustain". There can be little doubt that as *tang* means "to bear" because the 丈 *dang* "staff" which strikes is used to carry articles as a shoulder pole, so *k'am* means to bear because it is connected with 杠 *kang* "a pole used in carrying, to carry". In both cases the noise of collision originates a verb "to strike" *tang*, *k'am*, and a noun, the instrument *chang*, *keng* or *king*, "that which beats". It also originates *tang* 'bear", *k'am* "bear".

Any stem or upright long bone may be *heng* or *king* 梗, whether the bone of the leg, or the trunk of a tree, or a spoon used in stirring broth. "To pass" is 經 *ching* which is another way of saying *heng*. The oar by which boats are propelled is called *tsiang*

because it heats the water. In thus collecting some of the derivatives
of the one verb "to strike", we have seen exemplified the number
and variety of possible letter changes through which the root may
pass. But they might be easily increased if we included for instance
chung "bell", *ling-tang* "hand bell", and many more words originating in the sound of collision. We might select words ending in
n, such as 分 *fen* "divide", 頒 *pan* "distribute", 半 *pan* "half"
判 *p'an* "cut in half", 斷 *twan* "cut", 叚 "a cut off piece", 刊
k'an "to cut", 看 *k'an* "see", 見 *chien, kien* "see, perceive", 觀
kwan "see, look at". All these and many more with final *n* may
come from the same root "to strike", the original final *m* having
changed to *n*. We might then point to 鑑 *kam, kien* "see",
"mirror", as an example of the original root *kam* "to see", also
occurring in 賢 *lam* "to see", with the initial changed. Seeing
is distinguishing, and we distinguish by dividing.

The preceding case of *bam* "to strike", with this long variety
of changes embraces the whole period since the first formation of
the root and it is not surprising if during the thousands of years
which have since passed away the root should be metamorphosed in
a very high degree. But if we simply fix our thoughts on one
thousand years, what do we see within what is a comparatively
brief period? The changes are numerous, but they do not take
such extended leaps as in earlier times. Within 1000 or 1200
years we have the upgrowth of the Mandarin language. The
voiced shut consonants have been changed for the unvoiced and for
aspirates. Many words have changed *m* for *w* and *p* for *f*, but
such changes as from *p* to *t* and to *g*, do not occur. Thus we
learn that the farther we go back in the history of the language, the
more striking and revolutionary are the letter changes. Slight
transitions satisfy modern speakers. In ancient times it was not so.

On the whole all researches bring us back at last to the lip letters and to unity.

The direction of change has usually been from the lips and teeth inwards, but not exclusively. A few examples of change of *p* and *m* to *t*, *s*, *sh*, and *k* will help to make this principle more intelligible to any who may not be satisfied of the existence of the law. "Even", 平 *p'ing*, *bing*, 等 *teng*. "Bright", 炳 *ping*, 明 *ming*, 亮 *liang*, 光 *kwang* "light". "Comet" *p'ei*, *sui*, 彗 *hwei*. "Brush" *fu*, *shwa*, *sau*, 彗 *hwei*. "Behind" 背 *pei* "back", 北 *pei* "north", 朔 *so* "north", 後 *heu* "behind". "Side", *p'ang*, *bang*, 棱 *leng* "side of a table, of a cube etc", *kiang* "boundary". "Return" 反 *fan*, 轉 *chwen* "turn", 還 *hwan* "return". *Fan* is in fact the same as 變 *pien* "to change", and possibly may be the hand turned over, or a derivative from *p'an* "to grind, revolve". Another instance is 卑 *pei*, 低 *ti*, 下 *hia*, each meaning "low". Now it appears to be sufficiently ascertained that in former times the change was from without inwards, so that *p* or *m* became *t* or *n*, and *t* or *n* became *k*, *h* or *ng*. Thus *ming* "bright" might become *ping*. It might also easily become *ning*, as may be judged by the fact that at Shanghai *wei* "tail" is *ni*, although the old sound is *mi*. This may be illustrated by the story of the Fuchow servant who was sent to buy some *yang mei*, his master meaning the arbutus fruit then in the market. Instead of this he brought sheep's tails *yang wei*. His master excused him because he himself had used a wrong tone in pronouncing *wei* "tail" which is in the rising tone and in Fuchow is called *mui*.

The change of *ni* to *dz* may be illustrated by the word 靜 *dzing* "quiet" from 寧 *ning*. *Ning* is a common classical word while *dzing* is occasionally classical but chiefly a modern word. The initial *ni* in 人 *nin* "man" and other words changed to *zhi* about

A. D. 1000. When the characters were made, 果 the character for fruit would be called *da* or *na*. It is now *kwo*. How do we know that the old sound was *da*? In reply it may be said that this with twenty or more other phonetics in common use have the initial *l* or *k*. All such phonetics must have had when first written the initial from which the letter *l* has been evolved. This would be *d*, or *n*.

On the opposite side of this question allusion may here be made to examples shewing that the direction of change is sometimes from the throat outwards. For example when *k* becomes *ch* and when *sh* or *h* becomes *f*, this is the case. Thus *c'he* "cart" was anciently *ku*, and *chu* "dwell" was anciently *ku* also.

Guided by these facts we may conclude that labial initials and finals met with in Chinese words are relics of primitive times, while the other letters are of later origin and have been evolved from the labials. Gutturals have been formed by evolution from labials or from tooth letters. The letters which the tongue makes by approaching the palate were formerly evolved from tooth letters, but more recently from gutturals. The law of evolution is from without inwards and instances disagreeing with this law are exceptional.

Old words in Corean and Japanese should be compared with Chinese words under the light of the law of evolution. For example Japanese *idzumi* "fountain", Corean *suim* "well", are doubtless the Chinese 井 *tsing*, old sound *tsim*.

There are instances of change from final *m* to *p*, of final *n* to *t* and of final *ng* to *k*. Thus *san* and *sat* both mean "to scatter". The labial initial *p* occurs in *po* "sprinkle, winnow" and in *pan* "distribute", *fen* "divide". The real root is the hand because we have also *fang* "to let go", which is reducible to a root *pam*. The adjective *loan* "disorganized", is simply *san* "scattered", with the initial changed. This example seems to show that *san* is older than *sat* and that the order of derivation is from *n* to *t* and not from *t* to *n*.

The point of departure was the lips and the direction of change was from the lips inward. From this it follows that etymologies are to be sought in labial forms. Thus we ask what is the origin of the words for "constant". We have *p'ing*, *siün*, *ch'ang* and *heng*. The answer must be that *p'ing* "even" is the source of all these words. No other etymology is likely to be right.

The proofs of change from labial initial to dental and guttural initial, may be regarded as six. 1. Phonetics. The phonetic 勺 has the value *piau* and *cho*. 婦 *foo*, *bu* "woman" with bamboo radical is *sau* "sweep, brush". 黑 "black" is *hak* or *mak*. I omit for brevity twenty or more other phonetics which might be adduced. 2. Since final *m* changes to *ng*, *n*, *p*, and final *p* to *t* and *k* as the dialects shew, the initials *m* and *p* may also have gone through the same changes at an earlier stage. 3. The great number of cases that may be adduced where the meaning and final agree and the initial differs requires the acceptance of a law of change in initials. 4. The uniformitarianism of nature is opposed to separate origins for roots with dental and guttural initials when one labial root is enough. 5. Physiologically there is no greater difficulty in passing from *b* to *d* than from *b* to *v* and *f*, and the great length of time during which the Chinese language has lasted would easily allow of interchange between such well defined letters as the labials, dentals and gutturals, now being considered. 6. Physiology shews that the lips are so well supplied with muscles and with blood, so flexible, so capable of assuming the tight configuration which the vowel *v* and the labials require, that as wordmakers they would naturally precede all the stiffer vocal organs.

VI.

Since gesture preceded the language of the voice it is necessary to consider what gestures could be transferred and made permanent in human language. These were chiefly three, those of the mouth, the hand and the foot.

The *mouth gestures* would embrace as one prominent feature the act of shutting the aperture by pressing the lips together. This made the letters *m*, *b*, and afterwards *p*. In addition to this the same gesture might serve to indicate silence, swallowing, disappearance, concealment, burying, bringing to a close, dumbness etc. Such incipient words would take *m* as their final, and in the first instance *b* or *m* as their initial. The opening of the lips would conveniently represent the act of asking for food, the feeling of hunger and some other ideas, and it will be observed that while the mere opening of the lips helps to make no lip consonants, it aids the vowels greatly. This gesture is necessary for the sound of *a* in particular, and in fact for all the letters except the lip consonants. The infant to receive nutriment rounds its lips, and in speaking they are rounded also for the sound of *o*, one of the oldest vowels. In "Visible Speech" the author shews how the width of the lip aperture is varied so as to pronounce what he calls the high, middle and low vowels whether primary, or wide. The upper lip moves but does not descend because the jaw is fixed. The lower lip goes down to the greatest extent when the vowels in psalm, on, all, man, are pronounced. It falls to a less extent for the enunciation of the vowels in *up*, *ask*, *high*, *door*, *home*. It goes down to the least extent when the vowels in *eel*, *ill* are heard. It is not the lips only that become wider and narrower to make vowels, there is a corresponding expansion and contraction of the voice channel within the lips back to the throat and this is effected by the tongue. At first a few vowels would suffice and they would be attained by successive attempts to imitate the vowel sounds in nature. These by the three successive widenings of the lips would be *a*, *i* and *o* only.

Interjections are the language of the feelings. They are not words; yet the use of the voice in interjections would involve in each of them a more or less definite configuration of the mouth. They are such as *a*, *ha*, *ya*, *o*, *ho*. Feelings of joy and grief are expressed by certain muscular movements attended by sounds which might become words.

The *hand* is used in striking or in pointing. But pointing having no sound would take its vocal representation from the act of striking. Let us suppose that it was *ba*, *bam* or *bab*. This would in the first instance represent the hand, the implement used by the hand in striking, the act of striking or pointing, and the person struck or pointed at. Here we have in a rudimentary form two nouns, a verb and a pronoun. Subsequently distinctions would be made by help of the existing three vowels and labial consonants aided by gestures and each of the nouns, and other words would gradually acquire a sound peculiar to itself. When labials proved insufficient the tooth letters would be added to the stock.

At the same time the formation of words expressive of pulling and pushing, driving and leading, pointing to the right and left, before and behind, above and below, throwing, scattering, embracing, cutting, moulding things into shape and a hundred other actions of the hands would each be on the path towards an earlier or later completion. In the formation of words for all these ideas separate roots would not be needed. They would be derivatives and these derivatives would not be formed as in polysyllabic languages by adding syllables, but by modifications in the monosyllabic base. The modern word *mai* "to buy and sell" which has been already referred to is a case in point. "To sell" is *mai* in the departing tone. This sense originated in the period when this tone was in course of formation. The new derivative took the material which was supplied by its environment. It first occurs in the Chan-kwo-ts'e, a work of the 3ᵈ century before Christ. The departing tone was then about to appear. A new sense to a word requires a new peculiarity of sound to mark it and this was afforded by the new tone. The meaning "to buy" occurs also for the first time in the history Chan-kwo-ts'e and in a contemporary author Han-fei-tsï. It is therefore quite clear that *mai* "buy" and *mai* "sell" were then two words newly formed from one and distinguished only by tone. We seek for their root in 貿 *meu* "trade". This is an old word which means exchange, and like 易 *yi* and other common words having this sense, can be best referred to the action of the hands in changing the place of things for its origin, because the traffickers would in negotiation necessarily use their hands a good deal in showing what they meant. A root meaning hand was taken as the name.

The use of the *foot* in gesture language while more limited than that of the hand would also be not small. The operations of stamping, kicking, running, walking are all attended by noise. These indefinite sounds cannot be successfully imitated by the voice so that they shall take the form of distinct words. But men did what was possible for them to do. They took a root *ba, bap,* or *bam,* and to this they added a modifying peculiarity for each special sense. They took some piece of the material, whether labials, vowels, or gestures existing in their environment and with it modified the word they already had. What they did with *meu* "to trade" in order to make it into *mai* and *mai* "buy" and "sell" two thousand years ago, they also did a long time before with words meaning "foot" or "walking" for example. They formed them by letter changes one after another into words each expressing some action of the foot. What was accomplished by a change of intonation in modern times was accomplished by letter changes in very ancient times.

It does not appear that the gestures however expressive made with the help of the eye, chin, head, shoulders, neck, were capable of being utilized in the formation of words. They were not accompanied by sounds.

A sound was needed as a base. To this it was necessary to add some new peculiarity which was supplied by the lips, the teeth, tongue, palate or other organs. The new peculiarity once added the word was competent for a place in the vocabulary, if accepted by the people.

In imitating sounds heard in nature whether those of cutting, striking and hammering or the call of birds and other animals, the vowels of the voice are more near to the sound than the consonants. Thus *a* in the crow's note, *i* in the hinny of horses, *u* in the call of doves would be so reproduced anywhere. But in regard to the initial consonant the human imitator would take *b* or *m* uniformly in the first instance because the lips were in gesture making already in active use and *m* and *b* were easy to produce.

The aid afforded by sounds is plainly indicated by the feebleness of the eye as a helper in word making. Words of seeing are reducible to words of cutting. Thus 見 *chien* "to distinguish objects, to see", is best explained as derived ultimately from 辨 *pien* "distinguish", which is originally a verb "to cut".

Words needed something to make them current and permanent. What was it ? It was the differentiating element. Without this they would be like fading leaves falling in clouds to the ground. What made them *seeds* which could take root and exert a living power ? It was the *special sound* given to each when they were launched into life. This sound went subsequently through many changes till words reached their present form. The hidden capabilities of the voice were the reserve of power which the mind possessed. Each new idea had its symbol when required and it was the tendency to imitation which prompted the instinctive effort so to use the voice as to utter the appropriate symbol. *M* and *A* being the easiest letters come to be pronounced by the infant watching its mother's lips. *Ma* becomes the name of the object pictured on the retina; because *ma* is an easy sound to pronounce. The suppleness of the lips caused by their adaptation to take the infant's nutriment gives labials an advantage.

The mind was when in the infancy of language constantly feeling so to speak for a word. If no sound presented itself suitable to represent the idea which the mind desired to name, the hand or foot or the implement held by the hand, would supply the want. But if there were a sound it would be used for the required name so far as it could be successfully imitated. The sound would be combined with the name of the hand.

Words which are names of common objects of interest to the observer would be first formed. Those which describe frequent acts of the hand would especially be among the earliest. *The necessity of distinguishing between what belongs to me and what belongs to another would force the demonstrative pronouns into existence.* Adjectives could not be far behind, because they express opposite qualities. The hand would be actively engaged in all such cases in intensifying contrasts and thus pushing forward the origin of words.

Where there is a significant gesture there is the germ of a word. In any natural sound we have nutriment which may help the new word to germinate. The idea is mental and stands first in order. The gesture comes next, and it suggests the name of the hand as a sign for the idea. Some natural sound attending the action acts as a guide to the lips in uttering some cry of the nature of a word. That utterance makes the word, which thus consists of four parts contributed by the mind, the hand, the natural object causing vibrations in the air, and the lips. The word however can only enter the conventional vocabulary of a tribe by repetition, by use in the hearing of others and by such modifications in the uttered sound as are needed for intelligibility.

The crow's call is *a*. Men hear it as *caw* or *ka*. In old Chinese it is 烏 *o* "black". In modern Chinese it is *kwa*. It may be *Kraehe*, or *corvus* or *korax*, or *goreb*. The *k* prefixed indicates that *k* was a favourite initial at the time when any nation adopted it in the name of this bird. The names *fu*, *mu* "father, mother" were probably *ba*, *ma*, and belong to the labial period in Chinese. The words *ta* or *dap* "to step", *tseu*, *tsok* "to walk", have received their initials in the dental period. The old form would be *bap*. Easy sounds formed the first words, and the first persons recognized by children learning to speak naturally took as their names the first distinct utterances from the children's lips. The cuckoo is heard in China as in Europe and is called Pookoo. The Chinese name is just as good an imitation of the bird's call as the English. Both *p* and *c* are added to the natural sound.

The natural sound must be added to the name of the hand or other intermediate agent to make the word. In the acts of grinding, shaking, falling, weeping, laughing, shouting, whispering, there is in each case a sound which the wordmaker in the primeval ages heard as we hear it. Love presses close, and therefore it is *ai* which means both things. Fear leads men to tremble, and *chan*, *king*, *k'ung*, mean both to fear and to tremble. There can be no doubt then that natural sounds are a part of words. So in Chinese "to search" is the noise made by a pole striking the bottom in lake or river. "To come" is the sound of approaching feet, and "going" is that of travellers departing. As the difference in the ideas is in direction, the hand must have pointed and occasioned by its intervention a difference in the roots. Should no sound be heard the mind gives the name of the hand to the idea, unless some associated idea suggests an appropriate name. Should the name of the hand be adopted some modification in sound will give it currency. Words have their source both in the imitation of natural sounds and in the varied and efficient activity of the hand which aided the mind greatly in the first progress of language. In the formation of the demonstrative the name of the hand is made the pronoun because it is also the verb "to point".

We may without hesitation accept this view of the imitation of natural sounds, notwithstanding the impossibility of reproducing them fully. The mind has resources to compensate for the deficiency in the admirable variety of vowels and consonants producible by the vocal organs. The produced word is far better than any facsimile of the natural sound would be because the wordmaker when using his stock of sounds uses them under the control of a law. The vowels and consonants form a system of sounds organically connected. What began with the imitation of inarticulate nature ends with an admission to a place in the organic creations of language.

Nor need we be afraid that if the labial vowels and consonants were the whole stock of letters at the commencement of language that the number of words would be too limited. Words are made one by one by derivation, and they are still being made after so long a time has elapsed since language commenced its career. As soon as a need of new letters was felt they would be added with the aid of the tongue and teeth. The power of changing one letter into another is a faculty of the mind which is constantly in exercise. The vocal organs are so constructed as to admit of this easy transition. The lower lip for instance can touch the upper teeth. This makes *f* and *v*. The tongue by touching the upper teeth makes *d* and *t*. The closing of the lips may be changed for the shutting of the tooth barrier by the tongue. This act gives new words beginning with *d*, *t*, and *n* for old ones beginning with *b*, *p*, and *m*. By varying the mode in which the tongue is applied to the gums and palate *l* and the sibilants are formed. All these and the other letters being produced by slightly shifting the lips and tongue it is reasonable to expect that new words would be originated by a slight shifting movement as they were required. Thus "to send out" is *fang*. "Let go" is *p'ing*, old sound *bang*. It is changed from *bam* "the hand" because the stretched out hand points in the direction of the sending. *Fang* comes to mean "place", and also "square" because the hand can point to the north, south, east and west. *F* changes to *h*, and we have *hiang* "direction, directed towards, a general name for place, village". If *f* is replaced by the original *p* we have *pang* "a list, written from right to left in columns". *Fam* "a mould, pattern". *Ch'wang* "a square frame of wood work". *K'wang* "a square basket, eye socket, door frame, window frame". *Siang* "box". *Lung* "cage".

Even before the tooth letters were taken, there were twenty seven syllables without counting *p* as distinct from *b* and much may be done with a syllabary of twenty seven and unlimited gestures to boot. A labial period might exist for a long time with this stock. Letters slipped from the lips inward to make new letters as they were required.

Most words were formed not by independent creation but by derivation. The reason of this is that less effort is required to form a new word by derivation, and currency in the national vocabulary is more readily obtained for words originated in this way. When the new word is introduced the organs of the voice are already accustomed to produce certain sounds and this they do instinctively. Take as an example *feng* "to offer with the hands". Old sound *bang*. Two objects placed side by side are pictured by the hands so placed as in making a salutation. The root is *bam* "hand", and the natural sound imitated is the noise of collision. The pronunciation slips inward, and *ch'eng* 呈 is heard. The meaning becomes "offer gifts to a superior", the sound slips to the back of the tongue, and 貢 *kung* is " to offer tribute". There is but one root to these words. It is useless to search anywhere but in the labial word for the true root. The claims to the honour of originating this group of words seem to lie between *feng* "join the hands in offering", *p'eng* "meet in collision with noise" and *p'ang* "side". But in fact the hand "*bam*" and the noise of collision combine to form the root, the word *feng* is still a derivative, and hand "*bam*" is the root.

Our philology is much simplified by reducing almost all roots to the class of derivatives, and this is required by the law of least exertion. The multitude of speakers who learned to make the transition from *feng* to *c'heng* and to *kung* found the task easy because it was only the initial that needed change.

Among the modifications which are used to mark new words *aspiration* is important. It existed before the invention of the

characters,.for many words in the oldest records have it. It was much used in new derivatives. For instance a verb *pun* "to divide" is in existence. Another word with peculiarities of meaning as for example "cut in two with a knife" is required. The way chosen to effect this modification in sense is to aspirate the initial and retain the root. The result is *p'an* with an aspirate attached to the labial check *p*. *Economy of energy* marks this mode of making new words.

Independent creation of roots in language being unnecessary is extremely unlikely. Derivation from a few labial roots requiring but little exertion to pronounce them is sufficient to account for the growth of the Chinese vocabulary.

Gesture alone could never have been expanded into language. But language was possible by effecting through the voice a transition from the communication of thought by gesture to speech as we know it. Men used gestures first and then learned to make words by imitating sounds. Gesture was therefore the precursor of language, and language took its place because it was capable of being brought to greater perfection as a mode of communicating thought than gesture ever could be. Gesture and language existed together in the early stages of language and gesture when it became unnecessary was abandoned through the operation of the law of least exertion.

A root sometimes joins another to make a new noun. An edible fungus used in Chinese cookery is called *mu er* "wood ear" because it resembles an ear and grows on certain trees. This is an example of late formation and of those compounds of two words, which very commonly occur in the modern language. It consists of species and genus, or of subject and attribute. If ear be taken as a class, wood marks the species. Or ear may be viewed as a part of the tree when the mind chooses tree as a starting point.

New words are the divided parts of old words. From *dap* "to step" come 走 *tseu* "to walk", 足 *tsok* "foot" and 蹶 or 蹄 *t'i* "hoof". All are named from the act of stepping which was *dap* as will be shown farther on. A hoof is a foot of a special shape and a certain modified pronunciation was set aside to describe it. Such a variation was the result of a law according to which a difference in sound accompanies a difference in sense.

If we look into the process here presented to us a little closely, we shall find that *tseu* the verb "walk" and *tsu, tsok* the noun "foot", were not allowed to remain long undivided. The mind decided to drop the final consonant when the idea was that of a verb, and for the time to retain it to mark the noun. Two words were thus formed out of one. The use of the word 腿 "thigh" for the whole leg suggests that this word also is a derivative from 足 *tsu*. We have too 趾 *chï* "sole" and 脚 *chiau, kiak* "foot". The final *k* in two of these words points to identity between them. Can we not also find a labial initial and final? It is not far to seek. The adjective "low" is 卑 *pei*, 低 *ti* or 下 *hia* and these may be considered as reducible to one word by making allowance for letter changes. *Pei* and *ti* have final *k* in their phonetics 白 *bak*, and 氏 *dik*. The foot would be used in the days of gesture language to indicate what is low. We have 底 *ti* "bottom", 蒂 *ti* "peduncle, stem, calyx, bracts". The word means all these things because the essential idea is the lower part of a flower, or branch. Another derivative is 地 *ti, da, dap*, "earth, the ground". Stamping with the foot would very naturally originate this word. Its phonetic 也 *ye* has final *p*. Placing these facts together we conclude that the original sound was *bap* and that all these words are derivatives exhibiting varying stages of letter change. The foot, here called *bap* from the noise of stamping, is wordmaker in this case in place of the hand which usually holds that honourable office.

The connection of gesture with language may be illustrated by the old practice of knocking the forehead against the ground. This is called 頓 *tun* 首 *sheu*. The oriental custom of prostration is thus expressed in old Chinese. *Tun* is "to strike against". In modern letter writing *tun sheu* is the equivalent of "yours respectfully". It is also used for nodding through drowsiness which is called *ta tun*. But nodding means assent also and the initial is changed to express this new idea as in 允 *yün*, 準 *chun*. The idea of fidelity in 信 *sin*, "trustworthy", "to trust", may be thus derived, and 殷 *yin* "real" for prostration was once the symbol of fidelity. The ease with which the prostration act can be imitated in its details, would materially assist in originating these and other derivatives. Many thousand years ago men would eagerly mimic the drowsy man's nodding and compare it with prostration to excite laughter in o'hers. Thus new words would originate.

Marks were made for some words even before the invention of writing. The numerals were marked by counters which were suggested by the fingers, for the fingers are counters and are the basis of decimal arithmetic. 知 *chï* "to know", 識 *shï, shik* "to know", 識 *chik* "make a mark", 記 *ki* "mark, remember", 畫 *hwa, gak* "mark, picture", 悉 *sik* "know", 哲 *chï* "sagacity", may be derivatives from a finger making a mark as a sign of knowledge. The name of the hand seems to be the root. The sound is *tik*. The mark is a dot or a down stroke. *Tik* has become 知 *chï* and 識 *shï*. Confucius said 默 而 識 之 *mak ni tik ti* "I secretly make a mental mark". This is what men did when they formed the Chinese words meaning to know. They used a finger as a sign, or they made a mark on the sand or set down a counter. This became to them the verb to know. In Amoy *chi* " know " is called *ti*, and this sound is a waymark by which we may learn the original form of the word.

VII.

PERIODS OF DEVELOPMENT.

The time for the first appearance of roots would be the labial age when gesture prevailed extensively and in the civilized period when the upgrowth of various arts originated many new words. During the same period the principles and usages of grammar would grow into authoritative shape. All this would happen before the invention of writing. At that time, B. C. 2500, we find that the arts of weaving, agriculture and astronomical observation were known, while the old grammar was fully developed. Let us call B. C. 5000 to 4000 the labial period, B. C. 4000 to 3000 the dental period and B. C. 3000 to 2000 the guttural period. When the characters were invented the guttural age was not finished for we find traces in the phonetic characters indicating this fact. Thus 劍 *chien*, kim, sword, has a phonetic which is pronounced *ts'ien*, and *lien* and which would be *dim* when the characters were made. The age of the two oldest tones extended from B. C. 2500 to 1800. The age of three tones reached from B. C. 1800 to B. C. 300. The age of four tones existed from B. C. 300 to A. D. 1000. The age of five tones commenced about A. D. 1000 and has continued till the present time.

The age of metallurgy gave occasion to the terms *twan, lien* 煆 鍊 to smelt, to refine. Perhaps they were derived from *pien*, to change, or from *fen* to burn. So 紡 *fang*, to spin, is probably derived from 放 *fang*, send out, and the idea of the word is lengthening. 織 *chï*, tak, to weave, is probably derived from the crossing of threads in weaving. It would be tap and from this tak would be derived. It is the same as 作 *tso*, tsak, make, do, which also means hand work, and that work is frequently done in lines crossing each other. Such words as these indicate that the period when the mechanical arts flourished was the period also when dental initials came into use. We find dental initials in 輪 *lun* wheel, *lun*, *chwen* revolve, 爐 *lu* stove. The arts of metallurgy and pottery would render illustrious the fourth millenium before Christ and open the way for the art of writing and of astronomical observation in the third millenium when music, navigation, metallurgy, and metrology were greatly expanded.

The new grammar, that of the mandarin language and the dialects, has been developed during the thousand years that have passed since the Tang dynasty. It is very remarkable how little trace of the mandarin grammar we can find before A. D. 1000. Can it have been that the creative genius that originates grammatical forms slumbered till then and awoke anew after an inactivity of three thousand years? Native scholars have searched industriously for examples of colloquial speech in the writings of the historians but have found none earlier than the 6th century. In the Sui shu we read 阿 娘 不 與 我 一 好 婦 女 亦 是 可 恨 "That a niang, my mother, should not give me a good wife is certainly detestable". The phraseology is thoroughly modern and colloquial in its spirit. This passage might be spoken on the stage now as mandarin of a somewhat old type. Chau yi, a critic of immense learning, vouches for there not being a sentence of modern colloquial speech in any of the early histories (1) yet in criminal cases at the present time the testimony of witnesses is not seldom given in its original colloquial form, in memorials laid before the throne. We may then conclude that the creating genius of the language only began in the fifth century to formulate the modern colloquial idiom. Its variety of word groups linked by agglutination are new but they are made chiefly after old models, Many hundreds of new groups of old words have been added to the already rich treasure of fixed phrases existing in the book language. Thus the mandarin speech and the local dialects have in modern times grown to their present shape.

In the Peking Gazette we meet with modern phrases such as 不 成 事 體 *pu c'heng shï t'i* for impropriety in action. The official style rests on the Book of History, the Shu ching. But it has newly coined phrases such as this which is scarcely more than two or three centuries old.

VIII.

CAUSES OF VARIATION IN WORDS.

New words are formed by derivation from older words. The mind influences the vocal organs and causes a change in pronunciation so as to suit a corresponding change in the idea. *Dom* is the immediate root of 量 *liang*, measure. *T'ung* is the form that *dom* takes when a barrel is thought of. The old sound was dom. It is a barrel, or a cylinder. A bamboo cylinder would be a very convenient measure in early times. *D* changes to *l* and final *m* to *ng*. The result is *liang* measurement, to measure, *liang*, grain, tribute in kind.

(1) See the work *Ke.yü tsung kau* published about 1780 by Chau yi.

These variations commence with the sporadic novelty of an individual, proceed from the individual to the locality, and from the locality extend through the nation. The changes which occur can only obtain firm hold on the language by the united effort of many persons. What we usually see is usage firmly fixed and marked by no variation. Speakers limit themselves to certain sounds and never think of departing from tradition. Yet a change enters, extends in spite of this conservatism and gradually prevails over a wide extent of country. To gain this triumph there must be the union of various persons, influenced by a *tendency to imitation* and unanimously accepting some change which occurs in the speech of an individual who is taken as a model.

In the Chinese language the tendencies to variation, are some what like the modifications we see in the vegetable world in endo gens, while the natural history of polysyllabic languages is rather like that of exogens. Monosyllabism is controlled by a limitation in form and area and all changes have a restricted range. The field of evolution is bounded by the monosyllabic limitation. The word grows inwards in monosyllabic languages and outwards in those of polysyllabic structure.

The desire to emphasize a *special sense* is the cause of an immense number of variations. The verb tung, to understand has been formed from *dung* 洞 "see clearly" by change from lower to upper series, that is to say, by change from the voiced to the unvoiced initial. Search in deep water is implied in the three dots on the left. The verb 從 *t'sung*, to follow, lower even tone, was formerly dzung. It became tsung with the departing tone with the sense follower. With the upper even tone it means footsteps. The word in the sense "vestiges" may originate in the root 範 *fan, bam*, model. 黥 ch'ing, to tattoo, make impressions. But the verb to follow would naturally be demonstrative in origin because the hand can point out the path followed.

(2) Variations are caused by the *weariness felt in constant repetition*. The people of a neighbourhood may long retain a particular configuration of the vocal organs, but after some decades of years they will certainly tire of it and a change will occur which will gradually become popular Such local changes are independent of special sense. They arise from a desire to modify the configuration of the organs. Consequently they occur contemporaneously in all the words which have that particular configuration. Thus the voiced consonants have about A. D. 1000 been abandoned in favour of the unvoiced in the whole country north of the Yang-tsze-kiang. At the same time that 平 bing became p'ing with an aspirate 同 doong also became toong with an aspirate. This was the rule in the even tone or p'ing sheng. In the other tones the unvoiced shut consonant without aspiration was uniformly adopted. Doong to move is never t'ung with an aspiration in mandarin because it has the departing tone. It is heard toong.

(3) This weariness springing from repetition explains the origin of such extensive changes as the universal abandonment of the voiced consonants in favour of the unvoiced, but when the change has been well inaugurated the imitative tendency inherent in the human species may be sufficient to explain its further extension. This tendency to imitation leads a son when he leaves his home and comes under other influences to modify his pronunciation quite unconsciously. A difference in the sound of certain words as pronounced by father and son may be noticed in China by the observant investigator, but he need not ask a son why he pronounces differently from his father for he will deny the fact from a sense of duty. The weariness of constant repetition shews itself to be

powerful as a destructive agency by dropping initial or final letters altogether. In the early stages of language the speaker was obliged to pronounce these letters and he made the effort for the sake of intelligibility but omitted them when he found that the muscular action they required could be curtailed without detriment to clearness. The speaker gains something if he can be intelligible for instance with a more aspiration instead of *k*. When letters are dropped there may be a curtailment of muscular action or a change in the muscles employed. When *man* " ten thousand " becomes *wan*, muscular closing of the lips is abandoned and the contraction of the sound passage by the lower lip and back of the tongue is substituted.

The *muscles find rest in change* as well as in ceasing to perform their habitual contractions and the Chinese language having gone through a very long history the number of variations in letters is remarkably great. In Canton many words that should have initial *h*, or *k* with the aspirate, take *f*. In Shensi f is heard for *sh* in very many words. In Fuchow final *k* is employed instead of final *t* and *p* which are quite lost. In Amoy final *t* is found for final *p* in some words. Yet in others the Amoy dialect has retained the ancient final *p* when in the Kwang yün dictionary of the 7th century *p* has been changed to *t*. In Fuchow the final letters *m* and *n* are exchanged uniformly for *ng*. These examples are sufficient to shew that in the caprices of dialects the most useful distinctions of sound may be recklessly sacrificed to save exertion. In Fuchow the final letters *t, p, n, m* are resigned without a sigh in order that the muscles may not be at the trouble of enunciating them. The consequence of this improvidence is that Chinese from a distance listen to the dialect as an unknown tongue. It should be added that variations are caused by *mountain ranges* which shut a people in and greatly diminish intercourse. In these circumstances accidental variations are easily exaggerated into differences so important that the brogue of a valley becomes almost another language.

A powerful cause of variation in language is the *limitation of the attention* to certain particulars in objects of thought. A new aspect is observed in the idea and this must be symbolized by a new modification in the sound. The new thought becomes both clearer and more limited in proportion to the attention given. The thinking of the mind closely exercised upon natural objects increases human knowledge and civilization advances. Every word descriptive of objects or acts comes to have a new and larger meaning, and usually a modification of the word will take place. Thus liang «good» is from the same root as *c'heng* 誠 sincere, 今 *ling*, good (honorific), 成 *ch'eng*, to complete, 整 *cheng*, complete, round, put in order 臧 *tsang*, good, 正 *cheng*, correct, 當 *tang* correct, befitting. One root originating these moral words may be tang that which is in front and has no onesidedness, that which is in the middle.

Limitation of sense is a cause of variation as in the following examples. To pierce is expressed by t'am. It may be pricking with a needle or breaking through with a blunt instrument, or cutting through with a sword. The instrument whether of iron, stone or wood draws to itself the mind's attention. A name is given to the implement and it is usually the same as the verb t'am which happens to be popular at the time. Thus tsam is hair pin, 鐕 *chim*, chen is needle or lancet 針, *t'sim*, *c'hien* is strip of bamboo 籤, tsam is a chisel or to chisel 鏨. The last of these words is used for engraving on copper or stone. The wants of man as artisan induce new variations in this way from the old word. The workman does not create a word from nothing. He modifies an old word and forms a derivative.

Let us take as an example t'sang, to hide. This is the same essentially as doong cave, and doong barrel. The sound heard through reverberation from the walls of a tubular interior is written as dom. It may be an echo or a musical sound.

The tubular space prolongs it and it becomes a word when imitated. To bury is tsang. Stolen property is tsang. The larger viscera of the body are called tsang as being store houses for certain things, and as being hidden from view. A granary is t'sang or lim. These special meanings attached to one old word, mark so many new derivatives, all within the limits of a monosyllable. In the polysyllabic languages of Europe derivatives are formed by adding syllables but not exclusively so. Life from live, tore from tear, and sarg, song from sing, are changes within the monsyllable, and are analogous to the mode of derivation in Chinese. We find tsang to bury in the book of history and conclude that while it is now in the departing tone it was originally in the even tone. Hence it was not by tone that it was first distinguished, but by initial. It was marked by the sibilant *ts* to distinguish it from *dz*. This was before the invention of writing, for then the *ts* phonetics already formed a distinct class by themselves. At that time tsang to bury and dzang to hide might very well coexist.

Civilization introduces words. Let us take a word from medicine. The Cheu li speaks of nine viscera and nine openings to the body. Let us suppose the date of the first use of tsang for the viscera to be B. C. 600. The sonant initial *dz* was used. The name being given shews that great attention was then bestowed on medicine, and indeed at the same time or later a large number of new medical terms appear in the native literature. This new vocabulary was the fruit of application of mind, bestowed at that time on a special branch of knowledge.

The *effect of fashion* on variation should be here noticed. Many changes in pronunciation take place without change in the idea. This is on account of sporadic variation which through *tendency to imitation* spreads like fashions in dress, in gardening, or in household economy, over a wide tract of country. If at such a time a variation in idea should occur the controlling mind would select the new pronunciation which was then in fashion to mark the variation. Thus 當 *tang* is to represent. The commercial idea to pledge and a pledge are derivative senses. They are marked by the departing tone.

Among causes of variation in words which should be carefully noted is that of *fancied cacophony*. There is no reason why *pap* should not be a good word. Some dialects of old Chinese have it, as the Corean dialect for example, in which, *fa*, *law*, is *pap*. Yet in many dialects *p* twice in the same word is not allowed. The latin *m* may be repeated as in *memoria*. It is cacophonous in Chinese and the last *m* is changed for *ng*. But in primitive Chinese it was quite possible for *m* to occur twice in the same word. The fear of cacophony sprang up in later times and varies according to the locality. It has originated most extensive changes.

Compensation is a law by which for instance if a final consonant is dropped a vowel becomes a diphthong to balance the loss.

Obsolete words become limited to use by readers who meet them in studying old books. Such words are *liable to special* laws of *variation* in sound. Some words are avoided by authors and remain in local speech. Such words come to be affected by local laws of variation. Thus dialects grow up. Often the reading pronunciation differs from the colloquial pronunciation. But local variations gradually disappear and the mandarin speech is always gaining in territorial extent upon the tract occupied by provincial dialects.

The reason of the victorious progress of mandarin is found in the influence of the court and the efforts made by all influential persons to strip their speech of provincialism as an aid in discharging their official duties. The custom of the country is for no one to take office in his own province and when an officer goes to the seat of his dignity he takes his own neighbours and friends with him as followers. This tends to diminish the influence of dialects.

The *honorific principle* has given occasion to the appearance of numberless words. It seeks to use a large variety of special phrases to honour kings and aristocratic persons. An immense number of words which would have become obsolete are kept in permanent use by this principle which insists on a distinction in speech according as the person spoken of is to be honoured or to be treated as a common man or as an inferior.

The causes of variation are, 1, imitation of sporadic novelties, 2, emphasis on special sense, 3, weariness of constant repetition, 4, rest sought in change, 5, limitation of the attention, 6, effect of fashion, 7, fancied cacophony, 8, civilization making new words, 9, honorific principle, 10, compensation, 11, phonetic decay resulting from the law of least exertion, 12, the shape of the mouth changing for one letter often affects its neighbour.

IX.

AGENCY OF THE HAND IN WORD MAKING ILLUSTRATED.

The letters pronounced with the lips being in an advantageous position for use in the formation of language we may suppose *bam* or *bap* to be the first Chinese word for hand or it may have been *ba*, or *ma*. The same would be the demonstrative. Through the great variety of dialects, and the great age of the language all sorts of changes have taken place and the sound of each word is in a state of uncertain flux.

The roots for pointing and the hand are

指 *chï tik*, to point, finger   示 *shï, zhi*, to point
臂 *pei, pak* arm   擘 *p'i*, thumb
手 *sheu*, hand   点 *tien, tim*, point

Some common actions performed with the hands are expressed by the following roots

播 *po, pat*, scatter   摩 *mo, ma*, rub, grind
執 *tip*, take hold of   把 *pa, pak*. hold.
據 *kü, kok*, hold   持 *c'hï, dik*, hold
拒 *kü, kok*, resist   拉 *la, lap*, draw
攝 *shep*, take hold   接 *tsip*, take with the hands
憑 *bing*, hold   推 *t'ui*, push
提 *di*, lift   押 *yap*, press down
幫 *pang, pam*, assist   綁 *pang, pam*, bind
放 *fang, pam*, let go   拘 *pau, pok*, hold in the arms.

Whenever the hand is prominent in acting, the name of the hand would naturally occur to the word maker. To this he would add a rough imitation of the sound of the action as in grinding. The frequency of *b, p,* and *m* in the preceding examples is remarkable. But *p* changes readily to *t*, and *t* changes readily to *s, sh* and *ch.* So too *p* and t change to *k* and *h* and it is by these changes that many words once having labial initials and finals have lost them.

The initial *sh* of 手 *sheu* hand is to be viewed as changed from *t*. This t occurs in the Amoy c'hiu, hand, and in the phonetic value tok of 寸 *t'sun*, inch, found in such words as 得 *tek* to get 肘 *cheu*, tok, elbow, 守, *sheu*, guard, 壽 *sheu*, dok, old age,

討 *t'au*, chastise. In all these words tok, or dok is the ultimate sound at which we arrive if we go back far enough. If we go back still farther we obtain 文 p'ok to strike lightly.

We must not separate the hand from the demonstrative, which it helps to form. *P* and *m* appear in 彼 *pi* 某 meu, 每 mei, 麼 mo. The reason that pi, that, the farther demonstrative is pi, and this, the nearer demonstrative, is ts'ï 此, is that pi was the older and was pushed out by the new comer, as the young cuckoo in the sparrow's nest pushes out the little sparrows soon after they are hatched, Ts'ï would be formed from di the Soochow demonstrative, this. When it appeared pi became that.

The history of tso left and yeu right was analogous to this. Tso or tsap would be the old word for the hand and it would be usually the right hand. Tsap. would be formed from tap and dap, for in Chinese surds are the offspring of sonants. When sheu came into use it pushed out tso which was then used for the left hand. The right hand needed a special mark and it dropped sh and became 右 yeu. The final p of tso is detected by comparing the characters in which it figures as a phonetic with words like them in sense and having final p. By continuing this process the name for right hand becomes dok or dik. The left hand would in the early stages of the language be without a special word, because it was not a powerful aid in word making like the right hand. The various energies of pointing, driving, pushing and the rest were all the acts of the two hands taken together or of the right hand only. The hand has also aided in making words to express the direction of movements and the position of objects in the space which surrounds the word maker. Words of outward motion and a position in front of the speaker would naturally originate in the forward motion of the hand or in simply pointing forwards. To stretch out is chan or chen or chang. Of these the primitive form was tam. Then we have six derivatives from tam, namely 張 chang, 展 chan, 伸 shen to stretch out and 前 dzin, 先 sin, 進 tsin. The adverb and adjective "before" is thus explained. Sien and tsin are two surd derivatives formed from the sonant dzin. The same root with m as initial appears in 面 mien, front, face.

The hand points back and helps to form 退 t'ui, go back, 後 heu, guk, behind, 背 pei, pak, back, 北 pei, pak, north. The origin of these words is in the name of the hand which points. Front would be first formed and when it took a tooth initial, the old demonstrative 彼 pi could be appropriated to express the sense behind. This seems to be the reason of the occurrence of p in back and north.

Special relations above and below obtained words to express them also with the assistance of the hand. To press down is gap. To press up or support above is t'ok.

To send out is fa, pat, 發, and also fang, pang 放. P has become h in 向 hiang, towards. Fang, square, a place, is the same word with hiang. Its original meaning is sending out. As there are four principal directions in which a messenger may be sent it became convenient to use fang in the sense square. Hiang a village is also the same word. It is the place towards which motion is directed. When the hand points out the direction of motion a clear picture is formed in the mind and it becomes natural to use the name of the hand as a word to express forward motion in the direction indicated. The soul calls for clearness of outline when it proceeds to make words. It advances from the clear to the obscure and from the near to the distant. Every new word formed in this way is a hand subjected to a fading process and then revivified in a new shape to suit some fresh phase in the thought of the period and form another addition to the vocabulary.

The idea of pushing upwards seems to be connected with the notion of upward motion generally. The hand in representing the idea of ascending motion or of an object being above another, may simply point upward or it may push upward. The word 托 tok is used for water bearing up solid objects on its surface. One of the words for ascend is also 陟 chï, tok, and we have too 舉 kü, chü, kuk, to lift. To float 浮 fu is probably of the same family. The hand pushing upward may have originated all such words, from its primeval form bap. While this took place the other form of the hand root, namely bam, may have originated those words ending in ng which indicate upward motion. They are such as shang, teng, cheng and feng, to elevate with the two hands, which last had a labial initial b or v the original of the modern f.

The idea of upward motion is made more complex by the circumstance that the body rising from a sitting attitude may have shared with the hand in the origination of the roots. We have for instance. 起 k'i, c'hi, rise and 興 hing, rise. These may be represented in gestures by the hand, the body, the head or even the foot. All we can say here appears to be that in word making in this case the hand would probably have the chief share. The chin or foot might be used in pointing, but these grotesque acts would prove abortive in making words. The absence of serious effort would be too obvious, and imitation would not be thought of. We still feel compelled to assign the honour of the chief place in word making as the mind's instrument to the hand alone.

The efficiency of the hand as the mind's chief aid in wordmaking would be much increased by the use of a staff for a certain class of ideas. A bow and arrows, a knife, a hatchet, a spear, a measuring rod multiply to a still larger extent the hand's efficiency.

The activities of the human hand are numberless and its importance in word-making is proportioned to those activities. The hand takes hold of things for instance to save them from danger. This idea is expressed by keu 鉤 keu a hook, or to hook. Of this word another form is 救 kieu, chieu to save. Also 搭 tap, unite by hooks as in erecting an awning, or tent, connect, with. Both these roots symbolize the hand taking hold as with a hook. So also in the word kieu save, there is an allusion to the act of the hand in the radical on the right, which is pok, to «rap» here used with the meaning hand. Another word for save, and also meaning pull up, is 拔 bat and it has the labial initial. T'ui 推 to push, select, is the action of the hand pushing from within outward or upward. It has the tooth initial, and is aspirated for intensity. The name of the hand and some natural sound make up this word. The hand drawing anything towards itself is 挽 wan 引 yin 援 yuen. The hand by its construction, being able to take hold of things firmly and draw them in any direction, the mind assigns the name of the hand to any such action. We know that final n is evolved from m and initial y from t, and thus we conclude the original form of this verb to have been tam from bam one of the hand roots. The wrist, wan, derives its name from its use in this action and on the other hand gives its name to measures. C'hi, tak, a foot, is the length of the hand and has no connection with the human foot. Metrology belongs to the dental age in Chinese development. Take as another example 托 t'ok used for the width of the stretched arms and the same as 包 pau, embrace. Both these words are derived from the hand.

For rubbing and touching we have 摸 fu, pok, touch, press down, soothe with the hand, mo, rub, feel, ya, gap, to press down with the hand, 擦 t'sa, rub, brush. This last at Shang-hai is k'a and it is a good example of the change of the tooth initial to a guttural in a limited locality. It appears in another form as 搓

t'so, rub betwen the hands. When the rubbing is done by the
hand with the aid of file, sand paper, or brush, there is a difference
in the instrument. But as the act is the same the name is retained.
It must however be slightly altered or it could not obtain currency
as a name. By some easy modification, the new word serves as a
sign of the sense newly given. So also the words for brush, and file
may be credibly referred to this origin. They are ultimately derived
from hand or from the verb to point, not without aid from the
natural sound. That the transition can be made without difficulty
from the old word to a new one with variation in sound and in
sense, is due to the mind's effort successfully made to limit its attention to certain particulars.

Since the labial root may be pap, pam, map or mam, we may
expect to find a series of derivatives from hand with m, n, and
ng as their final letters. This is the reason that ts'eng is also a
word for rubbing as in mo ts'eng. The final *ng* is from *m*. *Ts* is
from *t*. *T* is from *p*.

The evolution of the substantive verb, at least the most common one, should be traced through the sense straight, right, to the
original root, the hand. The substantive verb rests on the adjective
''right'' as its basis in this instance, for it is more abstract than
that word, and the abstract is born from the concrete. Pointing o-
riginates the notion of a straight line and then developes the idea of
right. The quality of crookedness developes its opposite, wrong.
The adverbs not, no, are expressed by pointing in the opposite direction. The mind directs the arm to point in opposite directions and thus is seen to possess in fact the power to form
grammatical opposites with sounds to mark them. From the hand
was regularly derived the substantive verb, which when developed
with the help often of two or even three roots was found to

exhibit just this opposition. In other words it is affirmative and negative. To say "it is right" is to say "it is". The verb "is" may be described as the verb "is right", in a more abstract stage. In Chinese the demonstrative pronoun 是 shĭ, means *right* and it may also be used for *it is*. Its opposite is 不, 非, pu, or fei, which are modifications of the farther demonstrative 彼 pi. There is just as good reason for tracing negatives to a pronominal origin as the substantive verb in its affirmative shape. In both cases it is an affair of pointing. While the hand points in the reverse direction the mind assigns the negative signification. The root in final p has originated the substantives verbs (1) and demonstratives. We may suppose that in affirming the mind would be better pleased with the sharper sound final p, or k to which it changed, than with m. Final m is better adapted for simple description which welcomes a prolonged nasal. Final m is very suitable *for taking and keeping hold of a thing*. We find it in bing, ping, (2) handle, hold in the hand, ping, weapon, and hence the holder of weapons, the soldier. Yet this opinion that final m suits words which express continued action must not be held too stiffly, because to hold in the hand is also chii or kok. But in predication it is clear that the mind avoided final m, and initial m also, and decidedly preferred p, t, and k as better suited by their sharp outline to realize its attitude of decision.

It may be stated on a principle that can scarcely be controverted that the mind in making and using two names for hand at first would be led to this variety by the prominence of quick decision in predicating and that of sweet and prolonged melody in description.

---

(1) 爲 是 乃 wei, shĭ, nai. Also 有 yeu to have, there is, it exists.
(2) 十 柄 ping, handle 憑 bing evidence, something held in the hand.

P, t, and k, are suited for commands and assertions, while m, n and ng are adapted for unaccentuated narrative.

X.

NOUNS AND VERBS.

The parts of speech known as nouns and verbs are in the first instance not divided. Thus food and to eat are one thing to the mind when first observing. The hand places food in the mouth. The ear hears a sound of eating. The eye has seen the food. The nerves of taste and smell give additional information to the mind. A word bam or bap would be made. As a substantive this would be food. As a verb it would be to eat. The letters b, m, a, would be adopted because they are all easy to pronounce. The final m would mark the continued sound of eating and be partly imitative. Final p or b would mark a sound closed rapidly, and would also be imitative. The root was bam or bap at first. It became 食 zhik, by change of letters and this was the form when the character was invented. But there were at that time also 焦 tsiau, 茹 ju, and later there was 吃 k'iak, which ultimately became c'hï. The word 飯 fan, ban, rice, food, is a derivative from bam food. Final n is changed from m. There is no essential difference between verb and noun in these cases. But when the mind desires sharpness of idea, a special modification in the sound is added.

The primary identity or rather chaotic mixture of noun and verb is unquestionable. Reason extracted them from the phenomena in which they lay mixed. This may be seen in the words used for measuring. We have a labial root in 卜 pok, to guess at. We also have 度 tu, dok, estimate, measure, 揣 ch'wai, guess, 猜

t'sai, guess. The guttural forms are 估 ku, to estimate, 揆 k'wei, guess at. There are also several words formed from the root ending in a nasal, as 量 liang, estimate, measure, 付 t'sun to guess at, 想 siang, think of. Here the root with final k twice occurring meant probably tapping with the hand or with some implement and would be called bap. From this the words just mentioned with vowel finals would be formed. The fact that the hand and arm are used as measures would give the hand and the names by which it was known a preponderance of influence which would powerfully tend to lend currency to certain forms among those specified. Chang, a measure of ten feet, was a long staff such as would be used in bearing burdens. Ch'i 尺 t'ak, a foot, is the hand. It was anciently not more than eight English inches in length. There was a time when 尺 c'hï foot was the same with sheu hand and tu to measure.

The need felt for subdivision led to one word becoming a verb to estimate, another word a foot measure, and a third some other verb. The nasal ending attached to substantives like chang or verbs like liang to measure, is changed from the primitive final m. Words used as measures have usually dental initials and perhaps this shews that they were formed in the age of growing civilization which we may call the second or dental period of word creation. The mind saw before it a carrying pole tam, and proceeded to think of it as having a certain length. Time effected changes and it became dong and afterwards chang a measure of ten feet in length. It was further thought of as tam a weight sufficient for one man to carry. Then tam came to have this sense and to mean 100 lbs. Tam therefore means a load, a cwt, a carrying pole, and to carry. This is sufficient proof that verbs and nouns are simply branches from one root.

Verbs branch out also into various subordinate species. To walk, to stamp, to run, to leap, are one word originally. We find the word 踢 dap with labial final, to step. We also have 走 tseu to walk, 跑 p'au, to run, 涉 shep, pass a ford, 躐 liep, to stride, leap, hunt. The longer root bam is represented by 行 hing, to walk, formerly gang. In the classics we have 駟 馬 旁 旁 si me bang bang, four horses running. Here the primitive initial h is retained. To arrive at a place is also derived from the same verb. Thus 甫 fu, an adverb for «just reached», 赴 fu, arrive at, 至 chï, 到 tau, 低 ti, 及 gip, chi, arrive, are all referable to this root. So it is with the adverbs 方 fang, 剛 kang, just at that time. They are to be explained as coming from bam, fang, belonging to the late labial period and kang to the guttural period. The noise of the foot striking the ground may be credibly supposed to have originated all these verbs and verbal derivatives.

The words for falling afford a convenient illustration. The oldest is 崩 peng, fall heavily. Since it became archaic it has been used solely of the emperor's death. Falling is seen by the eye and heard by the ear. It must then at first have been imitative. Knowing what we now do of the laws of change in Chinese sounds, to what ultimate form can we reduce this very ancient word so suitably and with so much probability as to bam ? The later words which occur are 坍 t'an 傾 c'hing, and kiang or chiang to fall. But the first change of bam would be into bap and this is the root of lok, chui, tik, tiet, all meaning to fall. Their present form is the outcome of many ages of constant use on the tongues of a very active minded people. The root has therefore lost its primitive appearance. Such examples show how the history of words may be simply that of unity subdividing into ten thousand branches. From whichever branch we begin our inquiries we end in one common root, which was of necessity labial.

Another point to be here noted is that all verbs are nouns. A verb is a word, a thing, and as such it is a substantive. Chinese verbs are all capable of being declined. They take the form of a gerund or of an English present participle 我說無用 wo shwo wu yung, my speaking is of no use. 喫完 c'hĭ wan, finished eating. Such examples shew us the verb in its old state still unvivified by the greater vital force of Indo European or Semitic grammar. Chinese verbs have the marks of primitive antiquity. They are without sharply defined tenses such as aorists and futures. Nor are they furnished with inflections for the persons or to distinguish moods. Chinese verbs are unchiselled fragments, fresh from the quarry. That force of the mind which creates inflections belongs to words in a later stage among people of a more vigorous imagination. In Greek the clearness of outline in aorist tenses is very remarkable and is due to mental vigour and extraordinary creativeness The Latin verb has more of the substantive in its conception and form than the Greek has. The Chinese verb in this respect is more like the Latin. Every verb takes the possessive case after it and is rather declined than conjugated.

The evolution of the Chinese verb is the first great step made in the path of development of the grammar of actions. The root is in this case some action. The Chinese grammar treats the action as a noun with movement, in space and in time. It obtains a transitive force when a noun follows. Thus jen ch'i ma, man ride horse. Here are two nouns and an action. The picture on the retina gives information of this. The mind then creates in the verb a transitive force in accordance with the observed fact. Thus c'hi to ride becomes transitive as the effect of the mind's thought. It is the gift of reason that enables the soul to do this. The Mongol grammar is very different. Hwun mori onina, man horse rides The noun in the accusative is in the middle of the sentence. The verb

oni has a present tense termination. To account for these peculiarities possessed by the Tartar language we must suppose a prehistoric
mixture of races resulting in increased vigour which led to the inversion of the order of words and a system of tense suffixes. The
absence of such inversions and tense suffixes as occur in Tartar and
Dravidian languages justifies the view that the Chinese is more
primitive than any of these languages.' Inversions in the order of
words are unnatural and therefore not primeval. In accounting for
the evolution of the Chinese language our task is the easier just
because of the absence of such inversions, and the fact that the
order of words accords with that of the phœnomena which they
represent.

The simplicity of the Chinese verb may be illustrated by the
formation of the causative. the passive and the instrumental auxiliaries.

The *causative verbs* 俾 pei, 令 ling, 使 shï, 致 chï may be
traced ultimately to the demonstrative or the hand. Their differences in form are caused by letter change and by the constant
effort of the mind to attach to words certain minute modifications
in sense. Pei is to give and the phonetic 白 has a final k. Giving and causing are both expressed by stretching out the hand and
the name of the hand or of the demonstrative is assigned to the act.
The word ling command is simply a sound, the sound which gave
the command when the word was first made. Ling is from ding,
dom, bom, by the usual process which exists in modern time as a
relic of what took place anciently. The effect witnessed takes as
its name the sound heard. The words 使 shï, send, 致 chï may be
identified with 發 pat, send out. Sending is changed to causing
just as giving is changed to causing. The origin of all these words
is in pointing and they are separate branches from one primitive'

root of some early time when men gave attention to a certain sound they heard and while they pointed in the direction from which it came imitated it with that very small stock of letters they were then able to employ. There is no good reason why we should not identify these words with the early demonstratives 時 zhik and 彼 pak. The phonetic of 施 shï another word for giving, has traces in it of a final p. If we miss the original labials in one word we find them in another. The initial lip letter of liug « command » is found in ming « command ».

The mental activity which originated the causatives was at work long before the invention of the characters, for in the oldest literary fragments the causatives exist, but since that period the process of taking words from the vocabulary and giving them a causative sense has continued without interruption to the present time. The favorite modern causative is 教 chiau. This effect is produced by many uniting in a common aim, and through a long period controlling unconsciously the meaning of words so as to impart to them gradually a new signification.

The *passive* as a mode is not in the mind, but the power to make it is there. The Chinese use as passives the words 被 pei, 經 ching, 挨 ngai, 受 sheu, 蒙 meng. Pei and meng mean to cover. Ching is to pass over. Ngai is to come into close contact. Sheu is to receive. The phonetic indicates final k in 受 sheu and in 被 pei. The mind has metamorphosed these words into signs of the passive at different periods in the history of the language.

In 被 責 pei tse, to be beaten, we have an example of order inverted. To beat, tse, old sound tak, is a transitive verb and should stand before the person beaten. The mind however chooses to make the object nominative and searches for some word such as "receive" "suffer" which may follow the nominative and take the word beat as its accusative. Pei is the passive auxiliary and tse is a verb treated as a noun in the accusative. What is chiefly to be noticed here is the power exercised by the human will over the materials of language, which are moulded to its use as they are required. No grammatical forms are originally in the mind and when the mind manufactures them it is always by taking common words, depriving them of a large part of their signification and assigning to them a special use. Roots are in no sense a part of the original furniture of the mind. There is a profuse supply of materials at its disposal and these are shaped and trimmed till they acquire an aptitude for the special use to which by the mind's selection they are destined.

The *instrumental* auxiliaries are yi in the book language, and 把 pa and 將 tsiang in the colloquial. The first of these is perhaps 握 wok, take in the hand. Pa is the same in sense. Tsiang to lead is the same as ling which is the hand used in pulling or leading. E. G. 把那人治死 pa na jen chǐ sǐ, he put that man to death, or more paraphrastically, he took that man and put him to death by legal process. Clauses are subordinate or final. The instrumental particle with its substantive forms a subordinate clause followed by the principal verb in the indicative. The indicative always stands last. The voice marks by emphasis the principal verb. The instrumental verb is passed over lightly.

The auxiliaries of the *past tense* are in the old language 己 yi, 業 ye, gep, 既 chi, ki, all meaning already, past. These words would be verbs meaning to finish, from the act of cutting. The modern language has taken other words in place of these such as 了 liau 過 kwo meaning to finish, to pass. To *yi* is added 經 king, ching, to pass.

Nouns are in the old language furnished with a few *case par-*

ticles in the form of prepositions. The words 於 yii, at, used for the dative and locative cases, 在 tsai at, locative, are alike in their use and would very probably be the same word originally because the hand can by pointing supply their place. They would therefore be demonstrative in the first instance.

In the time of the earliest Chinese literature there was then the locative with a preposition to mark it. The instrumental also was marked by certain verbs as above stated. This shews plainly that if we judge by the literary remains of four thousand years ago, nouns were up to that time joined by agglutination, and very slight use was made of case particles. The possessive 之 chï was sparingly used. It was a demonstrative changed to a possessive by gradual use and was probably called tik. The frequency with which 於 yü occurs at that distant period indicates how stroug is the tendency in the most agglutinative languages to change some veɪb into a locative preposition and how early this tendency is felt

The substantive verb is the hand pointing.

The negative is the hand pointing in the opposite direction.

The causative is the hand giving and sending.

The passive is the hand covering or passing.

The instrumental is the hand taking.

The locative is the hand pointing.

Gesture maintained some temporary connection between the hand and these derivatives at first, but this would disappear as soon as they lost their concrete sense and became formal.

The development of the instrumental had proceeded so far that in the beginning of the Book of History we find that 以 yi which was originally a verb "take" had come to be used in the sense (as Legge (1) gives, it) "and thence proceeded to", or as it may be

(1) Legge Shoo king p. 17, 20.

taken "and so was able to". The wise king Yau had made his virtue conspicuous and thus provided went on to the love of the nine classes of his kindred. The word yi is both a conjunction "and" in this case, and an adverb implying the sense "from this he went on to". But the more common sense of yi in this ancient document is, in order to, as "in order to fix the central point of summer". Here we can see the nature of the instrumentality. It is the observation just mentioned of the meridian star which to their eternal honour the astronomers of that ancient time were able to make. By comparing these two uses of the instrumental particle in this, which in one of the oldest documents in the world, we can gauge the progress made at that time in developing the instrumental. We may note that it was an age when the interrogative and negative modes of speech were thoroughly current, and only the relative pronoun was rather behindhand in its growth.

XI

ADJECTIVES.

Adjectives are closely connected with verbs and nouns. For example 白 pe, bak, white, is really a word for light. Light appears when a hole is pierced in a wall. To pierce is ts'e or ts'ak. The labial initial if restored gives bak white. We have also feng for abundant which with the initials l, sh, and h becomes lung, sheng, hing, the last of which is both a verb to rise and an adjective prosperous.

Adjectives are usually in pairs. When direction is indicated by adjectives verbs of motion are involved in the idea. The hand indicates direction by pointing in the case of above, upper, below, right, left, front, back. The idea may become also an adverb or a postposition. It is so with 上 shang, ascend above, upper, with 中 chung, to strike the middle, central, middle, within. Beside the natural sounds imitated, the hand itself would be so important a factor that its name would inevitably enter into the composition of many of these words, to a greater or less degree. Right and left would be named from the act of pointing. The hand in a perpendicular attitude would give origin to the words 豎 shu, upright 縱 tsung, perpendicular, 樹 shu, tree, 柱 chu pillar, 祖 ancestral tablet and others. The hand pointing horizontally would originate 橫 heng, horizontal. The hand when pointing forward would become 前 c'hien, front, 先 sien, before, preceding. The hand pointing back would become pei, pak, back, and later it would originate 後 heu, guk, behind. Pei, north, anciently pak, is of the same origin. In 南 nam, south, two ideas inhere, The direction comes from the hand pointing south. But there is probably the idea of warmth included, and 炎 yen, yem, dam, flaming, hot, is possibly the word the sense of which has become entwined with the hand in making this root. High and low are expressed by pointing. Hence 高 kau, kok. 尊 tsun, 卓 cho, tok, 貴 kwei, kok, 崇 ch'ung, dom, 僑 c'hiau, gok, all mean high, while 卑 pei, 低 ti, 下 bia, ge, mean low. Two roots, one with final k for p, and the other with final m appear here. The name of the foot is included in the root for low because it gives a sound, and there is evidence of this connection in the fact that 足 tsok, 脚 chiau, kiak, foot, 底 ti, sole of the foot, closely resemble ti low, in sound and meaning. The words for high, probably include as an element kak, horn, the horn of the cow, deer, and other animals, when the form has final k or a vowel. Those which have a nasal ending may include the sense of the verb stretch *chang*, the arm being stretched upward to represent height.

The words 明 ming, 克 liang. 朗 lang and 炳 ping all meaning bright may be derived from a fissure or cleft, 縫 feng, hong, hom. With the same root 通 t'ung, penetrating, permeating and perhaps 清 t'sing, c'hing, clear, may be connected.

Words meaning dark or misty 暗 am, ngan, dark, 盲 meng, blind, 夢 meng, dream, 昏 hwun, dusky, muddy, appear to be all derived from the hands covering something, a sense expressed by mom, but the lips in this instance may just as well express the sense by gesture. While the lips were in succession closed, opened and closed again, there was an expulsion of breath and a vowel inserted.

Words expressive of the senses, blunt, rough, wild and disobliging, are likely to originate in a root meaning to resist which is found in tang to resist with the connected root dik to oppose. We find man, slow, man, wild and intractable, tun, blunt, c'hi, slow, wan, perverse, lan, indolent.

The idea of the beautiful seems to come from softness and a slight and graceful shape. Mei, beautiful, and mei the plum which is named from it are distinguished only by tone. When the rising tone began to appear 3600 years ago the word beautiful took a new intonation to define the adjective as a distinct thing from the noun. The plum flower has given a name to the chain of mountains between Canton and the provinces of Hunan and Kiangsi. The great fame of the flower only dates from A. D. 300. After this time it began to be a very favorite subject for painters and poets and was known as the queen of flowers. But though the flower is extremely pretty, bursts into pink and white blossom in the early spring each year, and has a delicious fragrance, it may have been from the fruit that it received the name mei beautiful, for strawberries and raspberries are also called mei, so that mei means sweet and soft. With a change of initial we have 弱 jo, nok, soft, 柔 jeu, soft, 姣 kiau, chiau, pretty.

All those adjectives which refer to space must have originated with the demonstrative, or with the hand.

All those adjectives which describe colours are borrowed from the names of coloured objects, Hwang, yellow, is from kim gold. Lam, blue, is from the sky. Lii or lok, green, is from soft herbs. 赤 ch'Y or tak, red, is from flesh 肉 jeu, nok. Hung, red, is from t'ung, copper. Hek 黑 black is from the crow. Wu, 烏 a classical word for black is also from the same bird.

Most of the other adjectives are metamorphosed from actions. Dim to sink originates shim, shen, deep. Hwo, living, is from hwo, move, shake. Tung, east, means rising. Si, west, is falling. Nam, south, is the hand stretched in front.

All those adjectives which imply reality and the sense of belonging to, are derived from the act of affirming, 實 zhet, real, is the same as 是 zhik, to be, and 有 yeu, it is so. All the three words mean the hand pointing. Perhaps hi 繫 tie, attached to, consequences, and 屬 shu, zhok, connected with, belong to, may be so explained.

Adjectives being the names of qualities are nouns. The eye sees colour before the mind becomes conscious of the presence of the object to which the colour belongs. Therefore the adjective stands before the substantive which it qualifies. The simplicity of Chinese construction does not allow of the adjective following the substantive, except where it is the predicate in a sentence.

The Chinese mind in comparing two things does not insert the substantive verb and lengthen the quality which is observed to differ by adding a syllable such as er, as we do. Thus, John is taller than William. The form is " John compare William tall ".

Hence there is no need of a comparative or superlative suffix.

Yet adverbs for more and most are commonly prefixed to adjectives. For more 愈 yü, good, surpassing, go beyond, is used. It is perhaps the same as piau and wai, outside, and is derived from a labial root attended by the act of the hand stretched out in front to picture something going past another thing. The word keng more is the same as tseng and tiem, to add, and if we go farther back we have meng, mom, to cover. Adding is expressed by the hands covering the object to which addition is made and thus the name of the joined hands becomes the root.

The superlative adverbs for most are verbs of cutting 極 chi, gik 絶 dzit, chiöh, or of arriving, 至 chï. Cutting and walking both have natural sounds which must have entered into the composition of these roots. While the adverb was still a verb, the adjective was a substantive. The change of the verb into an adverb helped to change the noun into an adjective.

XII.

THE NUMERALS.

The first efforts of man to count would be with the fingers. But these were not named separately, and we must look elsewhere for the origin of the numbers one to ten.

Of all the ten, the last is the easiest to explain. Shï 十 is in the old language, zhip, and this is a bundle or collection. We have 集 dzip, to collect, and 束 shok is to bind. We have it with a labial initial also, namely 縛 fu, bok to bind. Ten then means a bundle and the fingers limit the number in the bundle to ten. Final k is from p.

With this explanation before us it is quite clear that the makers of the Chinese numerals had counters. They used sticks or slips of some kind and they tied them together in bundles to count with and to use in divination. This was the beginning of their rude arithmetic. At present the Chinese in counting begin with the right hand thumb and end with the little finger of the left hand. Ten is the symbol of completeness because it is the number of the fingers.

If the Chinese had counting sticks when they named unity, a name for counter would become a name for one. A counter is 籌 c'heu, dok. We have 第 dik 祇 ch'ï 特 dek 獨 dok, all meaning only. This seems to suggest that — yi, called chit at Amoy, the universal word in Chinese for one, may be the name of a counter and contemporaneous with the words for " only " just mentioned.

We have a labial initial in 維 惟 vi, mi, wei, only, for which initial m occurs in the Fuchow dialect. The name dok for counter would be a word for cutting in the first instance.

But one may have been named from pointing, and ch'ï to point, may be its root. The counter may have been named from the hand and the act of numbering may have thus originated. That is —, 籌, 數, 指, yi, sheu, shu ch'ï may all come from the hand. The numbers two, four, five, and eight are the effects of division and the names for all these numbers might naturally be verbs to cut, modified.

Two, er or ni, would be to cut. The other words liang and shwang, a pair, are identical. For l and sh are both formed from d. 同 T'ung, dong is together, the same, and so it comes to mean a pair, and two. The later root of 兩 liang, two, is then 同 t'ung, and the earlier 併 ping, which preserves the lip initial. As to 二 er, ni, if it does not derives its origin from a verb to cut in two, it may be changed from 對 tui, opposite, because the fore finger is opposite to the thumb.

Sam, three 三 may be formed from 中 chung, tang, the middle, originally tam. From this old word, sam, three, was formed by change of t to s. The reason is found in the position of the third finger, in the centre of the right hand. It is also probable that 同 dung, and 併 ping, together, have had an influence on the formation of sam, three, as earlier they assisted to make liang, two. But the chief influence would be tam, central, indicated by the third finger (1).

Four 四 si, would be 削 siak, to cut, because two cuts at right angles make four, and nothing would be more obvious to the mind on the watch for a name than the act by which four was made.

Eight 八 pat, is accounted for by the action of a verb pat to cut 別 pit, dividing some object into eight pieces.

Five 五 ngo, ngak, may be explained as a verb to cut 刻 k'ak. The bundle of ten is in five divided into two halves. But as the hands are usually the symbols of five and ten it is perhaps preferable to account for 五 wu, five, as 捂 wu, ngu, to oppose, resist, the two hands being so held as to represent this idea. The idea of opposite is restricted and modified by mental suggestion so that it takes the meaning five. If this etymology be correct the Chinese word for five would be formed in the guttural period. The corresponding dental and labial words are 抵 ti, oppose, 配 p'ei, to match, 拂 fut, oppose.

Six 六 lok, lieu, may mean an addition. It agrees in phonetic elements with 續 sii, zok, to add, in succession, succeed to. Lok means then an addition of one finger to the five of the right hand.

Sevent t'sit, c'hi. Beginning to count from the right thumb

(1) Dr. Koelle in " Etymology of Turkish numerals " explains three in this way. Jour. Asiat. Soc. 1884.

the forefinger of the left hand signifies seven. Perhaps it is named from the action of that finger in pressing and touching 切 t'sie, to touch, feel the pulse.

Nine, 九 ku, chieu. Probably this word means deficient or one short of ten. Deficient is c'hiüe 缺 k'iuet. From this chieu may have been formed.

Chinese like all other Asiatic languages spoken over wide areas had the decimal notation when the numerals were made, for each number from one to ten has a name. Yet some of these ten names may have been made before others. In the time of gestures two threes might be used for six, and five and two for seven, by the use of fingers, before lok and t'sit were in existence.

The word 算 swan, calculate, is plainly from unity expressed by tan, single, and is to be included wih 籤 c'him, counter, as alike derived from the hand. This root appears also as chwen and twan, solely. It may be taken from cutting and may be the same with twan, a cut off piece.

A hundred is 百 pe, pai, pak. This word is evidently 伯 pe, pak, chief. The 100th counter would be longer than the rest or viewed as such and would therefore be called pek, chief. This admitted, it shews that counters were in use when this name for hundred was formed.

千 C'hien, t'sin, a thousand. This is the leader, the foremost counter, 先 sien, first, before.

萬 Wan, man, ten thousand. This root means many, wide, full. From these meanings it is derived by limitation of sense, a strictly mental act.

億 Yi or ik, 100000. From tik, a mark. It is also 100.000. 000. The reason of the uncertainty in meaning is that the word in itself only means a mark and the mark may be moved.

兆 Chau, djau, 1.000.000. The yi multiplied by ten. This also means mark or sign, and the special sense in given by the mind.

These numbers are mentioned as early as B. C. 1800, so that they belong to the vocabulary of the ancient astronomy and mathematics of the Chinese.

The word counter 籌 c'heu, has been important as an element in making some words, as the verb 持 籌 c'hï c'heu, to calculate, to devise plans.

Ordinal numbers are expressed by prefixing the demonstrative 第 di to cardinal numbers, as 第 十 ti shï, the tenth. As th in the English ordinal is a demonstrative pronoun modified, so it is with the Chinese ordinal prefix ti. The word ti indicates position and is certainly a word of pointing, the pronoun di or 是 shï.

XIII.

ORIGIN OF THE PRONOUNS.

The demonstratives may be referred for their origin to the act of pointing. The instrument in pointing is however no other than the hand, which would early obtain a name on account of its activity in the language of gesture. The hand, the act of pointing, and the pronoun, would originally be represented by one word and this would probably be the imitation of the noise of striking, by means of the letters b, m, a. At first the need of the first and second personal pronouns would be less felt, because the two men conversing were present. The third personal pronoun would be sooner required because the person meant was absent.

One of the earliest words used as a demonstrative 彼 pi, has a labial initial and from this would be derived such verbs as fa, send, forth and pei, to give. Pi would change to meu 某, ti 第, tsï 兹, shï 是, and also to 其 c'hi or gi. These may be distinguished as the labial, the dental, the sibilant, the palatal, or the guttural demonstrative. Among these it is the palatal, che 這, that has succeeded in best maintaining its position as a modern colloquial word, as in che ko, this. The word ko is a connective also originally derived from the demonstrative. This is shewn by the fact that in some Chekiang dialects as at the city of Haining, ke go, does duty both for *this* and *that*. When the distinction of that from this is required the people there say ke deu ke go " that, " while ke deu means " that place "; Thus a polysyllable has pushed out 彼 pi. Che 這 this, is the same word with 者 che, he who, that which. The relative force is given to it by placing it at the end of a clause. So also it is the same with the possessive ti 的. The demonstrative gradually obtains the possessive and relative force as the result of its position after a noun. This is nearly parallel wih our possessive s with the apostrophe in English. The initial relative 所 so, " that which " is also a branch from the same root. A demonstrative preceded a noun as in 所種之米 so chung chï mi, the rice which was sown. Gradually it assumed the peculiar force of the relative. Mi is rice. Chung is to sow.

The demonstrative 伊 yi is 是 shi, or 此 t'sï, without the initial consonant. This seems probable because 引 yin chief, 引 yin, to lead, agree in sense with 線 sien, thread and may be viewed as derived from it. The change of s or t to y involved in this identification is what often takes place, as in yang from chang, to grow, to rear. Probably the change to y took place before t had changed to *s*. *T* was dropped and i inserted.

The mandarin 這 che, this, is formed from the old Soochow

第 di, this, by evolution of surd from sonant and of ch from t. The descending tone is retained. Soochow was colonized about B. C. 1200 and became historical about B. C. 500. The pronoun di may date from that time.

The indefinite pronoun 某 meu, « some one », is changed from the demonstrative and interrogative mo 麼. Mo was originally that, but the mind wanted an interrogative, and made use of this root to obtain it. Some time after it wanted an indefinite pronoun, some one, and again it made use of the demonstrative mo, which is in fact another form of 彼 pi, that.

The interrogative pronouns are merely modifications of the demonstrative, and it is easy to tell by the initial letter from which form of the demonstrative they have been evolved. Thus 誰 shui who? is derived from dok or 孰 zhok, and this is no other than the old classical 時 shï, this, anciently called zhik. So also 何 ho, what, is the demonstrative 其 c'hi, anciently gi. In the process of evolution no factors were present but the mind suggesting the interrogative sense, the hand pointing, the mouth uttering the demonstrative in process of transformation, and the listener who accepted the new meaning and gave his help to make it current.

When the question is asked how many? the demonstrative with initial g is employed; that is to say 其 gi, becomes 幾 ki with the rising tone. Mencius has 幾 日 ki nit « how many days ». The question how many persons or things is also often asked by putting the opposites in juxtaposition 多寡 to, kwa, many, few. The demonstrative 若 jo, nok, is interrogative or demonstrative as it is also in its modern form 那 na. The rising tone asks a question, which? The departing tone replies, that man or thing. With 千 kan following it, jo is either interrogative how many? or it means « several ».

The energy of the language forming faculty is very clearly seen in the transformations which have taken place in the pronouns. By the combined and unconscious efforts of many individuals, the interrogative, the indefinite, the relative varieties have all been formed from the demonstrative. This has been done by the mind alone with the aid of the hands and voice. These varieties would grow into existence by insensible degrees and could not be the achievement of one man or one generation. Thus che this, na that, are in the departing tone and belong to the age of that tone which embraces in part the mandarin period.

The first and second personal pronouns may be presumed to be of demonstrative origin, because the hand is freely used in pointing to the speaker himself or to the person addressed. The Mongol and Manchu bi, I, bida we, are a relic of the labial period. The Chinese words 余 yii, 我, 吾 wo, wu, I, 自 tsï, tsa, should be viewed as demonstratives. The correctness of this opinion is supported by the fact that 儂 nung is a form for the first personal pronoun in Kanghi, but at Shanghai it is the second, as it is also in the Odes, where for you, we have 戎 jung, Legge p. 497, pronounced nung.

Hence we may conclude also that 自 tsï, self, 己 ki, self, are sibilant and guttural forms of the demonstrative. In this case the demonstrative by a decision of the will, means the speaker himself, and the modern Chinese points his finger to his nose to indicate this. For anything we know to the contrary this gesture may be a relic of primitive antiquity.

The demonstrative, that is the name for hand, in its numerous metamorphoses sometimes becomes the name of the place pointed at. Ch'u place 處 is thus explained. While the hand points and the mouth utters instinctively the pronoun most suitable, the mind may proceed in the use of its creative faculty, so far to limit and realize the idea attached to the sound that the pronoun is't 此, or some other, becomes an abstract noun and useful addition to the vocabulary with the sense place. The Japanese have tokoro for place and the Mongols jug. The Japanese have also ba for place. Hence it may be conjectured that the Japanese and Chinese languages were in connection in the Chinese labial period, and that these two languages with the Mongol were in connection in the Chinese dental period. Of course it is also possible that the Japanese and Mongol languages have possessed an internal law of development like the Chinese and they may have evolved these words without foreign concurrence.

The pronoun may also become a verb. We have a noun c'hu, place, and we have also a verb chu, to dwell. The notion of long continuance is 'mental and is added to the demonstrative. The equivalent verb with initial k 居 kii or chii, to dwell, seems to be formed from the verb chu or from the demonstrative with k. The evolutionary process is continued one step more by inserting an aspirate and we obtain c'hu, to arrange, give a place to persons or things. The transitive verb comes out of the intransitive. This is a signal instance of the creativeness of the mind in its more vigorous attitudes. At the same time such an exercise of vigour is not rare. Thus one of the obsolete demonstratives is *an*, which appears in the interrogatives *an* and *yen* used for where and how. This very root appears an an adjective « at rest, » « quiet » and is also used as a pronoun for the first person I and as a verb to arrange. The intransitive notion «being at rest in a place» is metamorphosed into a transitive verb « to arrange things in their places. »

That the mind has this power of metamorphosing words is shown by the fact that all languages reveal this class of phenomena in their evolution.

The relative pronoun does not appear in distinct shape in the oldest documents. But we find it in the Song of the Five Sons purporting to belong to B. C. 2188, and in the next chapter in the history. The relative appears in these passages in the form 者 che, " that which " or " he who " at the end of a clause. Perhaps its being in both chapters is evidence of a great antiquity. The earliest form is wei jen shang che, " he who is above men ", that is the ruler of men. The demonstrative is placed below the noun to individualize and limit a compound phrase for ruler. This sort of relative construction is a step in advance of the phraseology in which it is imbedded. The oldest Chinese style presents words in a state of agglutination with a limited use of particles when compared either with the learned or with the colloquial Chinese of modern times. The tendency of modern style is to multiply words of form and attenuate the realism of ancient speech.

The relative may originate in the fading of the interrogative force. Shui 誰 was interrogative before it was relative, as it was demonstrative before it was interrogative. Before the interrogative was formed the only thing possible to do when a question was to be asked was to use the demonstrative. The listener at last becoming aware that it was used interrogatively gave it that sense and the speaker differentiated it by some modification in the sound. So was it also with the relative. The interrogative pronoun lost its interrogative force and the residuum of meaning became the relative. This is seen in the reply to the question what bird 何 鳥 ho niau? The answer may be 不 知 道 何 鳥 pu chī tau ho niau I, do not know what bird. Here the interrogative is no longer a question. It is a relative. The demonstrative from which 何 ho, what, has been formed is 其 gi, c'hi.

XIV.

ADVERBS, PREPOSITIONS AND CONJUNCTIONS.

The word how as a question is the same as "what kind?". It consists of the interrogative with some noun of shape or form. The colloquial tsen mo, how? is shen mo 甚 麼 what kind? changed in its orthography. Again shen is zhim an old demonstrative used interrogatively by the same mental power which formed 何 ho, what, from 其 gi, that. The noun mo or mok means mould, frame, and is reducible to *map* as yang, chwang, hing 形 all meaning shape, are reducible to *mam*. The last step in the process is to identify *map* and *mam* and thus we arrive at the beginning of the evolution, with the mind, the hand, the vocal organs and natural sounds, as the only factors active in originating words.

The heavenly bodies, with the hand to make divisions, supply words of time. The word day 日 ji is the sun. Month is the moon. The ideas daily, monthly, are simply the words day, month, and they are adverbs if the word following is a verb. The words shi 時 , hour, 分 fen, minute, 秒 miau, second, are all verbs of cutting. Heaven 天 t'ien, is best referred to tan, chan, to expand. It forms a name for *day*, and in modern Chinese becomes an adverb, daily, when it precedes a verb, as 天 天 來 t'ien t'ien lai, he comes daily. The form in old Chinese is 日 來 ji lai, comes daily.

Adjectives and verbs become adverbs by position as in 敬授 人 時 king sheu jen shi, reverentially give the people a knowledge of the seasons.

Prepositions are formed from verbs. For example 至 chĭ, 到 tau, 及 gip, 赴 fu, are the same word with 走 tseu, walk, which would originally have a labial initial and final, and had gone through so many changes, even before the invention of the characters, as not to be readily recognized. The substitutionary prepositions are evolved from the verb dak, to change. They are 代 tai and 替 t'i.

The conjunctions are also verbs or simple demonstratives. In 三百有六旬 san pak u lak zin, 360 days, the conjunction 有 yeu, is the hand with the initial letter lost. 有 yeu, was at first in the even tone and so also was the conjunction 又 yeu, and. When the departing tone was introduced 又 yeu, was employed for this conjunction.

XV.

THE SENTENCE.

In the communication of thought between the first men there would be no inversions of the natural order of words. The subject or nominative would precede the verb, and the verb would precede the object. The order is that of time. Since the quality of a thing is observed usually before the thing itself the quality or any special characteristic comes first both in primeval and in modern Chinese grammar. It is followed by general terms. The adjective precedes the substantive and species genus. When two or three verbs come together their order is that of time. The spirit of Chinese grammar is seen remarkably in its treatment of verbs as substantives.

The following examples from the beginning of the Book of History, the Shooking, will shew what the language was four thousand years ago. Speaking of the emperor Yau, the history say 克 明 俊 德 k'ak mang tson tek, he was able to display high virtue. K'ak "was able" is the present k'o 可 "may" much used in the modern language. Mang, bright, is here a verb, make brilliant. In the early state of language the adjective and verb were still undivided. The adjective tson, high, (the same as tsung and sung high, the finals n and ng being both derived from final m) precedes its substantive, virtue, tek, which is simply the verb tso, "make" treated as a noun with special sense "virtue" attached to it. Another sentence is 乃 命 羲 和 欽 若 昊 天 nai mang kai ga k'om nok go t'en. He then commanded Hi and Ho reverentially in accord with the wide heaven 曆 象 日 月 星 辰 敬 授 人 時 lik zong nit get sing zhin kang zhu nin zhik, to make a calendar and representations of the sun, moon, stars, and certain stellar bodies. Nai, an adverb, "then" is a demonstrative modified. Mang "command" is from mam sound, cry of animals, etc. Hi and Ho are the imperial astronomers. K'om, reverential, is from kung, join the hands as a salutation. Nok "agree with" is lai, lak, rely on, lean towards, an action of the hand or arm. In "wide heaven" the adjective precedes the substantive. Lik is to pass over in succession, calendar. Siang is image, representations of the heavenly bodies. The sun, moon and stars are in apposition without conjunctive particles. "Reverentially" is an adjective qualifying the verb to give. The verb "give" has a nearer and farther regimen "to men" "and the times for ploughing and sowing". The verb governs directly the persons who receive the gift. A dative as in western grammar is sometimes inserted as in 徧 于 群 神 pin yo gun zhin, he offered the sacrifice called pien "universal" to the multitude of spirits.

"The day is long" is rendered by 日 永 nit yong. "The meridian star is Antares" is simply 星 火 sing ha. A complete year consists of 366 day", is rendereds 朞三百有六旬有六日 ge sam pak u lak zin u lak nit. Here ge is a fixed time; u, to have, is the connective "and"; zin is ten days and is probably the same with ts'iuen, dzin, entire, in allusion to the ten fingers as a symbol for completeness.

The predicative sentence, the day is long, is simply day long. If we invert the order and say yong nit, a long day, we have the adjective preceding the substantive.

Subordinate clauses precede conclusive clauses, as in the sentence 以閏月定四時成歲 yi nun get dang si zhik ding sot, by means of the intercalary month fix the four seasons and complete the year. In this sentence the instrumental clause is introduced by yi 以, a word which may be identified with 伊 yi, that, being distinguished from it by an intonation. Both words are derived from the primitive word for the hand.

We cannot call these sentences examples of pure colloquial idiom for we may detect contractions made in the historiographer's office. Pien as a name of sacrifice, and c'hi as a name for the year viewed as a fixed period, are instances of this. But independently of this intermingling of a few words of the chancery, the syntax comes clearly out to view as it existed in the spoken idiom of the time.

The special quality of a thing precedes the thing itself because the mind first notices a part and then the whole. The subject of a sentence precedes that which is predicated of it because this is the order of ordinary thinking. Of that Semitic quality in language which first looks at the action and afterwards says who is the actor, the Chinese as a rule knows nothing, for the language is not more imaginative than the nation which made it and uses it.

The Chinese sentence takes the middle path. It does not reveal poetic instincts by placing the verb before its nominative, nor does it on the other hand place the verb at the end of a sentence after the word which it governs. This unimaginative characteristic of Tartar languages is the result of mental dulness and is alien to the Chinese mind, which has always encouraged industry and intellectual cultivation.

Nations whose life is a series of adventures among mountains and on the sea; and to whom war songs are a delight, exhibit imaginative characteristics in their languages such as the assignment of the first place to the verb. The life of nomades restricts the intellect within narrow limits and leads to that inversion by which the verb comes last in syntax. The Chinese people belong to the sober, middle class of nations. Steadily devoted to trading and the cultivation of the soil they are neither poetic nor dull. Consequently the order of their syntax is strictly that of nature and time.

XVI

LANGUAGE IS CHIEFLY THE WORK OF THE MIND.

The mind is the soul considered as the thinker, the observer seated in the brain and watching the outer world by means of eye and ear. The senses, the nerves, the muscles, the tongue, the lips, the larynx and the lungs were all made before the invention of language. Thus splendidly endowed by his Creator man proceeded to construct language. He was able to make words because he had at his command the vocal organs with their wonderful adaptability to become the medium of thought, and the hands with their multiform capacity for action. Language then could not have been formed unless mind had been given to man enabling him to make the higher use of these organs. Here then we have the evidence that the soul is a gift from God distinguishing man from the other creatures, and elevating him to a throne of superiority from which he exercises dominion over them all.

The view advanced by some modern thinkers that the endowment of reason was the result of language is untenable. Geiger says " language created reason. Before language man was irrational ". In this treatise I aim to shew that it was by the incessant activity of the mind in receiving the reports of the sensations, in directing the vocal apparatus of the mouth, and in wielding the powers of the hands that language was slowly evolved. The mind came first with its intellectual and spiritual faculties. Language came into existence afterwards. There is no doubt that Geiger is wrong here, because philosophy, literature, history and science are the later products of the same mental power which first made language. It is as unreasonable to place the appearance of reason after the formation of language as it would be to place it after the appearance of literature, philosophy and science. These, with language all come from the mind as the mind comes from God.

Yet the mind being complex it need not be said that it was as a whole bestowed by the Creator at one time. The more intelligent of the animals, especially among the vertebrata and articulata, possess intellectual faculties analogous to those of man. What ought to be contended for is that man has higher mental powers, which have made him capable of forming language and producing a literature with science and philosophy and which have also made him a religious being. The powers which did this for man were a divine gift bestowed on him previous to the formation of language and in these the animals did not share.

The divine gift of reason has assisted man to map out the categories of grammar. It has also aided him in developing moral ideas and words. Thus jen, benevolence, is from softness. Ai, love, is coming near to. T'sz, maternal affection, is a sigh. Ngi or yi, justice, is an act of cutting. Liang, honest and conscientious, is roundness. Chung, loyalty, is the heart with the idea attached of centrality. Liberality is width. Li, politeness, is represented by straight lines drawn parallel and not only down but across. Sing, moral nature, is that which is born or produced naturally. The good, mei, is that which is beautiful. Badness, ok, is that which is dirty. It may be confidently asked how could a merely animal intelligence thus obtain the habit of elevating itself into the realm of moral purity, and exhibit the power of reasoning from the material to the immaterial as the Chinese roots shew that primeval men did reason? The creation of the moral vocabulary is at once a proof of an ascending intelligence and of the possession of a gift which the most sagacious animals have never been supposed to share.

www.ingramcontent.com/pod-product-compliance
Lightning Source LLC
Chambersburg PA
CBHW022144020726
47496CB00008B/2551